PENGUIN WRITERS' GUIDES

How to Write Better English

Robert Allen is an experienced lexicographer and writer on a wide range of language issues. He edited the Pocket Oxford edition of *Fowler's Modern English Usage* and is editor-in-chief of the *Penguin English Dictionary*. He lives in Edinburgh.

The Penguin Writers' Guides

PENGUIN WRITERS' GUIDES

How to Write Better English

ROBERT ALLEN

PENGUIN BOOKS

PENGUIN BOOKS

Published by the Penguin Group
Penguin Books Ltd, 80 Strand, London WC2R 0RL, England
Penguin Group (USA) Inc., 375 Hudson Street, New York, New York 10014, USA
Penguin Group (Canada), 10 Alcorn Avenue, Toronto, Ontario, Canada M4V 3B2
(a division of Pearson Penguin Canada Inc.)
Penguin Ireland, 25 St Stephen's Green, Dublin 2, Ireland
(a division of Penguin Books Ltd)
Penguin Group (Australia), 250 Camberwell Road,
Camberwell, Victoria 3124, Australia (a division of Pearson Australia Group Pty Ltd)
Penguin Books India Pvt Ltd, 11 Community Centre,
Panchsheel Park, New Delhi – 110 017, India
Penguin Group (NZ), cnr Airborne and Rosedale Roads, Albany,
Auckland 1310, New Zealand (a division of Pearson New Zealand Ltd)
Penguin Books (South Africa) (Pty) Ltd, 24 Sturdee Avenue,
Rosebank 2196, South Africa

Penguin Books Ltd, Registered Offices: 80 Strand, London WC2R 0RL, England

www.penguin.com

First published 2005
1

Copyright © Robert Allen, 2005
All rights reserved

Extracts from *Guards! Guards!* by Terry Pratchett reproduced by permission
of Victor Gollancz Ltd; *Mr Enderby* by Anthony Burgess copyright
© Estate of Anthony Burgess; and *The Book and the Brotherhood*
by Irish Murdoch copyright © 1987, reprinted by kind permission of
the Estate of Iris Murdoch

The moral right of the author has been asserted

Set in 11/13 pt Adobe Minion
Typeset by Rowland Phototypesetting Ltd, Bury St Edmunds, Suffolk
Printed in England by Clays Ltd, St Ives plc

Contents

Preface

A book about writing better English is largely, but not entirely, a book about grammar, because grammar is the expression of the way a language works. In Britain since the 1970s, the teaching of English in schools has been in turmoil as different educational viewpoints have come and gone. Old grammatical models have been swept aside but nothing substantial has been put in their place. This leaves many people uncertain about the role of grammar in their language and afraid of having to face up to it. They shouldn't be. In fact, everyone knows a great deal more than they realize about the grammar of the language they speak as their mother tongue, and in this book I have tried to show how you can build on what you already know to write and speak better English for a wide range of purposes. As for 'not entirely', I have included advice on techniques for using English imaginatively and colourfully, taking the topic well beyond mere considerations of correctness, important though these are.

Writing this book has been a great pleasure for me and I would like to thank several people for their help and support: Anne Seaton, with whom I have had many stimulating and rewarding discussions about English and the way it is used, George Davidson, who has written companion books on spelling and punctuation in this series, and the publishers at Penguin, in particular Sophie Lazar, who read a first version of the book and made many suggestions that have enabled me to improve it in important ways. Finally, I must thank the copy-editor, Mark Handsley, who has greatly enhanced the organization and appearance of the text.

Robert Allen
Edinburgh, 2005

About this book

What you are looking for

This book is about writing better English, and also about speaking better English, because achieving the first will help you with the second. Since you have picked the book up – even if it belongs to someone else! – you are probably interested in using language and have some idea of what it is all about. Writing is important to all of us in our everyday lives, especially now with the increased use of word processing and the huge explosion of communication by the Internet and other electronic means. All the more reason to be sure we are making the best use of our language and getting the message across successfully.

These are probably the main areas of support that you are looking for in a book like this:

- understanding the grammar and working of English more fully, intimidating though they seem.
- coping with problem words and phrases.
- knowing what really matters: being able to distinguish important issues from mere fads and obsessions about language.
- above all, acquiring techniques for writing more clearly and effectively, and – when necessary – creatively: being able to write better English.

What is better English?

But what exactly is better English and how does it differ from bad English? How do writers achieve better English? Is it just a matter of knowing rules and grammar, or is there more to it? What is grammar, and who makes the rules?

Many people are alarmed at the word 'grammar', and are put off it by the fear that it is a set of complicated and difficult rules; but grammar is not as daunting as you might think. It is simply the ways in which words are used and the patterns of usage that have become established in the language over many centuries of use and change. People who know English use these patterns instinctively, as we shall see in the first section, and you will discover that you have a lot more grammar in your head than you realize.

To appreciate this you need to think about what language is and what it is for. If you speak a language you use certain devices and patterns intuitively. You don't have to stop and think about them (for most of the time at least) but can reproduce them instinctively. Here are a few simple examples of this:

• changes of word form: many words change their forms, e.g. nouns (naming words) when they refer to more than one (the plural, as in *houses* and *children*) and verbs when you say *he cooks* instead of *I cook*; and you know when to say *we are cooking* instead of the simpler form *we cook*. (This last distinction, incidentally, can cause big problems to learners of English.)
• word order: *The dog bit the man* and *The man bit the*

dog have very different meanings although the words used are exactly the same.
• fixed patterns: when you use adjectives (describing words), those referring to size come before those referring to colour: *a little green car* (not *a green little car*).
• irregular features: most verbs add -*ed* to refer to the past (*cook, cooked*; *land, landed*) but some can end in -*t* (*learn, learned* or *learnt*) and others change completely (*come, came*; *stand, stood*).

If you think about rules as patterns they seem much less daunting because many of them are already embedded in your mind and you use them instinctively. You can build on your instinctive knowledge of English to become more aware of the way it works and to make your use of language more effective and interesting. This is in essence what we mean by *good* English.

Nonetheless it would be foolish to pretend that writing is just a matter of instinct and that there are no problems along the way. There are indeed rules that people find difficult; and there are plenty of observers of the language ready and eager to tell you when – in their view – you've tripped up. Here are some common examples of the kinds of things that can cause uncertainty. Dealing with these by building on the grammar you already know will help you to express yourself clearly and unambiguously, making a favourable impression on your audience:

• confusing words that sound similar, such as *fortunate* (which means 'bringing good fortune, lucky') and *fortuitous* (which means 'occurring by chance').

• using a plural verb (as in *they look*) when a singular verb is needed (as in *she looks*), especially in long sentences in which the verb gets separated from its subject (the word that the verb is telling you about), e.g. in the badly formed sentence *I've come to ask them what their understanding of the changes are.*

• making a slip with verbs ending in *-ed* and *-ing* (called participles), producing results that are imprecise or even absurd: *Reduced to a pile of ashes, he gazed at the place where his house had been.*

• using incorrect forms, as in *between you and I* (the correct form is *between you and me*).

• producing unintentional ambiguity (statements with more than one possible meaning): *If visitors park cars here, they will be towed away.*

• overuse of sentence-fillers (*of course, really, indeed*) and clichés (*at the end of the day, conspicuous by their absence*, and so on), which can weaken the effect of your writing and distract and irritate your readers.

You also need to be aware of language 'superstitions', rules and pronouncements about usage that are not based on sound principle: for example, that *none* must be followed by a singular verb and that *different* always goes with *from*. (There is also the question of the split infinitive, in case you were wondering: more about that in due course.) Once we recognize and identify the genuine problems and traps that exist in speaking and writing good English, we are in a much better position to be vigilant and take steps to avoid them. This book will help you to do this and will provide you with some techniques.

But better English is not just about playing safe and avoiding pitfalls. There are tools and techniques that help you in positive ways: for example using vocabulary effectively, using figures of speech to enliven your writing, and building sentences in creative ways to convey your meaning more effectively. We shall be exploring these aspects of our language too.

How the book is organized

The approach this book takes is a practical one. It assumes that you want to write better English and that part of this need is to understand how English works. It is concerned less with stating rules (although there are rules) than with identifying common and recurring problems and trying to explain them.

• **Sections 1 and 2** look at the framework of English grammar, firstly at word level and then, in the second section, in terms of groups of words: the second section is called **sentence building** and offers help with putting words together to express facts, ideas, and situations in effective and interesting ways.

• **Section 3** is about meaning and the different ways of expressing this clearly, effectively, and interestingly, e.g. by avoiding overworked expressions and making good use of metaphor, figures of speech, and other creative techniques.

• **Section 4** deals with the social aspects of using language: the effects our writing has on the people who read it. This is an important area now that sensitivities about language and the way we express our ideas are so high.

• **Section 5** is a 'problems hitlist', an alphabetical list of words and phrases that cause particular problems, with advice on how to deal with them.

I have tried in this book to avoid confusing the reader with technical terms that may be unfamiliar, but it is impossible to write in any meaningful way about language without using a core set of terminology. I have tried to give as much help as possible along the way by adding a brief explanation of any term that might cause difficulties at the point where it is first used; and I have repeated these explanations at key points throughout the book. Also, there is a **Glossary** at the end of the book which lists all these terms together with fuller explanations.

Throughout the book points of grammar and usage are illustrated by example sentences. Most of these are taken from real usage, so that what is being commented on is English that has been written and put in the public domain in one form or another, whether in print or in electronic form. Much of this material has been drawn from language databases, most importantly the British National Corpus, an invaluable collection of current written and printed English collected by a consortium of publishers and educational institutions.

Attributed citations from writers of the present day and the past (e.g. from 19th-century fiction) illustrate opinions about usage and also provide instances of controversial or disputed usage that are older – and better established – than is commonly thought.

Three special symbols are used when different uses

are being contrasted with regard to their correctness
or suitability:

✓ denotes a correct or unexceptionable use.

✗ denotes an incorrect or widely disliked use.

? denotes a use that is questionable or one often
  frowned on.

This is a reference book, and as with all reference books
you should keep coming back to it when you need it.
You don't have to read it in one go (although you can
if you want to). Each section is self-sufficient and deals
with a particular aspect of writing better English. The
support material in the glossary, tables, and index will
enable you to home in on specific problems and issues
if that helps you best. You may well find it most
effective as a source of help when you are actually
involved in writing of some kind: CVs or business
reports, creative writing, or simply writing for your
own amusement.

Standard English

The guidance given here is based on British Standard
English, the form of English that has become established in Britain as the form for use in education,
communications, and officialdom. You find it everywhere: in schools, in newspapers and magazines, on
radio and television, in films, and in literature. It is
also the form used in teaching learners of English from
abroad. There are other varieties of English: regional
varieties, for example. These are in no way inferior to
Standard English; they exist alongside it.

Standard English does not equate with formal English. You should not confuse these different varieties with levels of formality, or what linguists call *register*. Even within Standard English there are different levels of formality reflected in the vocabulary, grammar, and style of the language used. Again it is not a question of superiority but of appropriateness: what is suited to a particular domain of language use. This subject is explored throughout the book. For example, in section 4 dealing with the social side of language, you will find tables that give equivalent words in different registers ranging from the formal and official to the informal and conversational. Each has its own place at the right time.

A language to enjoy

The English language is a tool for everyone to use, and like all tools there are different ways of using it for different purposes. You should never be intimidated by those who claim that the language is 'under attack' or 'being corrupted' or even 'polluted', as though it were some kind of organic substance being contaminated. People have been saying this kind of thing for centuries, but the language thrives. Enjoy it, and enjoy reading this book, which is there to help you.

1
Words: the building blocks of language

Gramer, the grounde of al.

William Langland, *The Vision of Piers Plowman*, 14c

I never made a mistake in grammar but once in my life and as soon as I done it I seen it.

Carl Sandburg, *The People, Yes*, 1936

Too much importance is still attached to grammarians' fetishes and too little to choosing right words. But we cannot have grammar jettisoned altogether; that would mean chaos.

Sir Ernest Gowers, *The Complete Plain Words*, 1954

This section and the next one are about grammar, because knowing good grammar is an important part of writing better English. In this section we will look at the ways in which words are used to express meaning and ideas, and in the next section we will see how you can combine words and phrases into sentences and paragraphs so as to put your thoughts and ideas into continuous writing.

What words do: wordclasses (or parts of speech)

It was just a mass of words. We hadn't the least idea of what a part of speech meant.

Stephen Leacock, *Here Are My Lectures*, 1938

Sentences are made up of words and phrases and clauses (groups of words including a verb). Words are the building blocks of language. It is difficult to say how many words there are in English, because it depends on exactly what you count: on whether, for example, you include so-called 'compound' words such as *chessboard*, *newspaper*, *dry-clean*, and *filling station*, which are formed by putting other words together as continuous words or with a hyphen or space. There are about half a million defined items in the *Oxford English Dictionary*, but these include archaic and obsolete words and other words that are not in ordinary use. A typical household or office dictionary such as the *Penguin English Dictionary* contains about a tenth of this number, and the average active vocabulary of an educated adult is normally reckoned to be about ten thousand words.

Before we look in more detail at the ways in which we can put sentences together, it will be helpful to list the different roles that individual words have. These roles are called parts of speech or wordclasses. If you think about what a typical sentence tells you, you can see the different roles that are needed. It normally tells you about a person or thing, and something that is happening or existing, and it might describe a person or thing in some way or tell you something about how or why or where or when something is happening. All these types of information are served by the different wordclasses. Here is a list of the main wordclasses:

nouns	words that name people and things	*machine, information, pleasure, sugar, Rashid, jellyfish, Paris*
verbs	words for actions and states	*arrive, carry, follow, irritate, loosen, remain, undo*
adjectives	words that describe	*bad, green, holy, oval, perfect, Russian, worse*
adverbs	words that tell you how, when, where, etc.	*badly, yesterday, inside, on* (as in *moving on*)
pronouns	words used in place of nouns	*he, she, it, we, us, you, they, ours, theirs*
prepositions	words that show position or time or other relations	*after* (as in *after dark*), *into, on* (as in *on the table*), *until* (as in *until Wednesday*), *without* (as in *without a doubt*)
conjunctions	linking words	*and, but, if, unless, until* (as in *wait until they come*)

interjections	words that are exclaimed	*ah!, no!, oops!*
determiners	words that specify the number or identity of nouns	*a, the, every, some*

Sometimes the same word exists in more than one part of speech: in the table *on* appears among both the adverbs and the prepositions, and *until* appears as a preposition and as a conjunction. There are many other examples: *adult* is a noun (as in *adults only*) and an adjective (as in *an adult point of view*); *fast* is an adjective (as in *a fast car*) and an adverb (as in *a car moving fast*); and *master* is a noun (as in *a dog and its master*), an adjective (as in *a master key*), and a verb (as in *to master a language*).

Knowing about nouns

Of course the great wastage is in the verbs and adjectives, but there are hundreds of nouns that can be got rid of as well.

George Orwell, *Nineteen Eighty-Four*, 1949

Nouns are words that name things: physical things that you can touch and see (called **concrete nouns**), and things that are ideas in the mind (called **abstract nouns**):

some concrete nouns	some abstract nouns
house	*happiness*
sky	*love*
cucumber	*size*
hand	*duty*
stone	*speed*

For guidance on avoiding overuse of abstract nouns, see section 4, p. 191.

One or more?

Nouns can name just one thing, as all the examples given in the table above do: these are **singular** nouns. Or they can name more than one thing: *houses, skies, hands, cucumbers*, and *duties* are all **plural** nouns. Nouns that can form plurals are called **countable**. In English, many nouns form their plurals by adding *-s* or *-es*, sometimes with a change to the stem of the word (e.g. *activity, activities*). However, some nouns form their plurals in other ways: for example *child, children* and *woman, women*. Others have plurals that are identical to the singular form: for example, *aircraft* and *series*, many animal names (e.g. *fish* and *sheep* – although except for *sheep* these also have forms in *-s* to denote a number of individuals, e.g. *fishes*), and nationality words ending in *-ese*, e.g. *Chinese* and *Portuguese*.

Some nouns do not have a plural, because their meaning makes this impossible. For example, you cannot normally refer to more than one *happiness*, so the form *happinesses* doesn't exist, except in special uses or for some special effect. Nouns like this are called **uncountable**. Generally speaking uncountable nouns and meanings are not used with the indefinite article *a* or *an*.

Other examples are *chaos, calm, safety*, and *laughter*. Most uncountable nouns are abstract nouns; proper nouns are also usually uncountable by their nature, since they refer to one specific person or thing. Some nouns can be countable in one meaning and uncountable in another:

noun	countable use	uncountable use
activity	*There are some lively* **activities** *to pursue.*	*Police* **activity** *increased.*
beauty	*She was a well-known local* **beauty**.	*a place of great* **beauty**
conflict	*He faced a new* **conflict** *of loyalties.*	*Most people would not choose to provoke* **conflict**.

There is another class of uncountable nouns, and these are often called **mass nouns** because they denote a mass of something, e.g. *bread, putty, steel, wine*. They are not completely uncountable because they do occasionally form plurals in a special meaning 'a type of –' or 'an amount of –'. For example, you can say *three beers* (= three glasses of beer) and *a wide choice of breads* (= types of bread).

When to use a capital letter

The nouns we have looked at so far all refer to something general and are not identifying a particular person, place, or thing; and when they are concrete nouns, they can refer to any example of the things they name: *hand* refers to anyone's hand, *cucumber* means any cucumber, and so on. Nouns of this type, which form the largest class of nouns, are called **common nouns.**

There is another kind of noun, which you spell with a capital initial letter and which refers to only one example of what it is naming. These are called **proper nouns.** Proper nouns are typically the names of people, places, and institutions (regarded broadly):

some proper nouns

people	places	institutions
Napoleon	*Tokyo*	*Concorde*
Hamlet	*Saturn*	*the Church*
Apollo	*the Netherlands*	*December*

The term is sometimes applied more broadly to other names spelt with a capital letter, including geographical and ethnic designations such as *Scandinavian* and *Inuit*, which behave like common nouns, e.g. in allowing the forms *a Scandinavian* and *the Inuit*. Some genuinely proper names can also behave like common nouns in certain uses, e.g. *a fine Turner* (= a painting by Turner) and *a collection of Turners* (plural), *another Olivier* (= an actor comparable to Olivier). In these uses you still need a capital initial letter. Personal names are also usually classed as proper nouns, although they can refer to more than one person, e.g. *Mary* (*which Mary do you mean?*).

Some common nouns are also spelt with a capital initial letter when they have a special meaning, e.g. nouns that refer to major institutions – such as *State*, *Government*, and *Church* – in addition to their general meanings. A *state* (with a small *s*) is the general word (as in *they arrived in a filthy state* and *we crossed the border into a neighbouring state*), whereas a *State* (with a capital *S*) is a political entity referring to a particular institution (as in *the State should answer to its citizens*). A *church* is a building or the people associated with it, whereas a *Church* (as in *the Catholic Church*) is a particular body of Christian belief. If you are writing about *the art of good government* or *the policies of a Labour government* you use a small *g*, but you use a capital *G* when you are referring to a particular set of politicians in power (as in *the Blair Government*).

Collective nouns

There are nouns in English that look singular (i.e. they don't end in *-s* or have a plural form like *children*) but refer to several people or things, and are logically therefore plural. Nouns of this type are called **collective** nouns. In particular, there is one type of collective noun that causes big problems even with native speakers of English. This is the type that refers to a group, usually of people: *army, audience, board, committee, family, government, party*. They are awkward because they can be treated as either singular or plural, depending on the emphasis:

*Ethiopia's army **is** immense.*
*The committee **looks** at the facts and **expresses** an opinion.*
*The government **has** to get **its** money from somewhere.*

In these sentences, *army*, *committee*, and *government* are regarded as single entities and so they are treated as singular nouns. But armies, committees, governments, and all the other bodies in the list consist of individuals, and so they can be regarded as logical plurals. Compare the following:

*The whole family **was devastated**.*
*The audience **were invited** to put questions to the speakers.*

Notice that the problem only arises with words that have different forms in the singular, to give the game away: the third person singular present of verbs, and pronouns and determiners such as *its* and *their*. In other types of sentence, there is no means of knowing whether the writer intends the collective noun to be singular or plural, because the forms of the other words are the same in both cases:

*Yesterday the government **defeated** an opposition censure motion.*
*The audience **will be** much larger on Saturday evening.*

When the noun is preceded by a singular determiner such as *a* or *an*, *each* or *every*, or *this*, it has to be treated as singular:

*Each crew **has** to check **its** own rig.*
*This new generation **has its** own values.*

But when the collective noun is in the form *a – of* (people or things), it is usually treated as a plural:

*A group of children **were playing** on a see-saw.*
*Only a handful of them **qualify** as refugees.*

A number of, the rest of

Similar to these are collective nouns indicating size or quantity, e.g. *number* and *rest*.

   A number of is normally treated as a plural:

A number of *partial explanations have been put forward.*

Rest is treated as singular when it refers to a single mass and plural when it refers to several people or things:

(singular) ***The rest** of the meal was uneatable.*
(plural) *Some of the tourists stayed in their hotel, but **the rest** were keen to venture out.*

The general rule in other cases is to treat a collective noun as singular when the emphasis is on the group as a whole and as plural when the emphasis is on the individuals that form the group. The choice affects the form of the following verb and any pronouns such as *he*, *she*, *they*, *their*, etc. that are used to refer to the noun:

(singular) *The jury retired at 11 a.m. this morning. **It** still hadn't reached **its** verdict by the time **it** was recalled at 5 p.m.*
(singular) *Remember to make adjustments when the audience **is** present.*
(singular) *The government **believes** that the opposition has produced no real alternatives to **its** deterrent policy.*

(plural) *The new generation of novelists **were** more inward-looking.*
(plural) *The crew **are** all amateurs and only half know how to sail.*
(plural) *The judiciary **were** forced to resort to legal fictions.*

You may have noticed that in the first of these examples in the first group the problem is not with the form of the verb, because *retired*, like all simple past forms, is the same in the singular and the plural. The same applies to verbs such as *can*, *should*, *will*, and *must*, which do not change even in the present tense. The problem arises with the continuation of the sentence, which involves choices between *it* and *they* and between *its* and *their*. The important thing is not to mix singular and plural in the same sentence. It is surprisingly easy to fall into this trap:

✗ *The whole family **was** devastated when **their** house was burgled.*

Here, we have either to change *their* to *its* (but *its* sounds odd when referring to people, as here) or change *was* to *were* (which works much better):

*The whole family **were** devastated when **their** house was burgled.*

Here is another example which changes its mind halfway through:

✗ *The Government **aims** to place the children at the heart of **their** education policy.* (The verb *aims* is singular, whereas *their* is plural.)

Here we have to say either:

(singular) *The Government **aims** to place the children at the heart of **its** education policy.*

or:

(plural) *The Government **aim** to place the children at the heart of **their** education policy.*

Collective nouns representing a large or indeterminate number of people, such as *government*, *mob*, and *staff*, are treated in British English as either singular or plural according to the sense, but in American English the singular is always used:

The Government has made plain that it will lay down minimum rates of benefit. (The emphasis is on the government as an entity.)
The Eurobank's staff pay no tax on their salaries. (The plural form *salaries* influences the choice, since *its salaries* would be awkward.)

Majority *and* minority

There are also words, such as *majority* and *minority*, that can behave like collective nouns while also having more straightforward meanings:

(singular) *I remain convinced that a democratic majority **exists** for higher spending on public services.*
(plural) *The majority of children at junior school **have** no concept of time or rushing.*
(plural) *Only a minority **pay** off their entire balance every month.*
(other meaning) *The Labour candidate's majority **was** increased by 20%.*

Names of countries often behave like collective nouns and can be followed by plural verbs when they refer to the people or representatives of the country (e.g. a sports team):

Germany [= the German team] *were in good form, winning 3–0 against France.*
Japan [= the representatives of Japan] *occupy the seats in front.*

Collective nouns for physical things
Other collective nouns refer to collections of physical objects and people (unlike *family* and *government*, which refer to the institutions as abstract entities). These are more straightforward because they are all either singular or plural (they cannot be both):

singular collective nouns	plural collective nouns
furniture	cattle
luggage	people
machinery	police

Litter and *luggage*: *collective nouns that are always singular*
With the singular type of collective noun, any verb that comes after them or any inflected word that goes with them, is singular in form (e.g. *this* and not *these*, *was* and not *were*):

This [✗ *these*] *luggage* ***was*** [✗ *were*] *put on board later.*
Most bathroom furniture ***is*** [✗ *are*] *now specified in metric.*

People and *police*: *collective nouns that are always plural*

With the plural type of collective noun, any associated words have to be plural (e.g. *many* and not *much*, *those* and not *that*):

*Draught cattle owned by households **were** more often subject to theft.*
***Many** people **agree** that some form of control is needed.*
*The agreement included an amnesty for **those** police involved in Aristide's overthrow.*

Notice that these nouns, whether they are grammatically singular or plural, are plural in meaning, and if you want to refer to a single item you have to say *a piece of luggage* or *a member of the police*.

Politics and *measles*: *plural nouns treated as singular*

Examples of these nouns are the names of branches of knowledge or science, such as *acoustics* and *mathematics*, names of activities such as *billiards*, *gymnastics*, and *politics*, and names of diseases such as *measles* and *mumps*. With these we have the same problem we saw just above, but in reverse: these are nouns that are plural in form but are treated as singular, either always or in some meanings.

***Linguistics looks** at what we actually say and write, and tries to explain why.*
*Don't let anyone say **politics is** not about personalities.*

Here, the plural nouns *linguistics* and *politics* are equivalent to the singular expression 'the subject of linguistics' and 'the topic of politics' (*subject* and *topic* being the 'notional' subjects); but plural agreement is called for in a sentence such as *Green politics are based on the belief that the earth's resources are finite*, where the word *politics* is equivalent to 'policies' and therefore has a plural force.

*The figures show that **measles is** on the increase.* (Here, *measles* is equivalent to the notional subject *disease* or *illness*.)

In more casual conversation, this pattern extends to other plurals:

*If he bought **a small chips**, he'd have enough for some chocolate too.* (Here, an expression such as *a bag of* or *a portion of* is implied as the notional subject.)
*Human rights **remains** a major issue.* (Here, the implied subject of the verb is *the issue* or *matter of human rights*.)

This data *or* these data?

Some plural nouns, such as *news*, *data*, and *agenda*, are now commonly treated as singular. Depending on their meaning, they are either countable nouns, which can be used with *a* or *an* and have plural forms, e.g. *agendas*, or mass nouns, which do not have a plural form but are used with words that are characteristic of singular number such as *this* and *much*:

Good news has also come from the government this week.
The Prime Minister has set himself a formidable agenda.

Data is regarded as a singular mass noun when the emphasis is on its collective or cumulative nature:

> *We need to be sure that our data is in a form that can be used by other institutions.*
> *This data helps the zoo provide the best environment possible for the animal.*
>
> *Data* still appears occasionally as a plural in some contexts where the individuality of the items of information is important, or when language purists insist on its full grammatical value, although it usually sounds awkward or affected:
>
> *Data have been obtained from some 1500 diary respondents.*
> *These data were stored on the large IBM installation.*

Kind of –, sort of –

For advice on *this/these kind/kinds of*, see **Building sentences**, p. 114.

Some plural words adopted unchanged from other languages (called **loanwords**), such as *spaghetti* and more recently *graffiti*, develop singular meanings as mass nouns:

The local police, against whom the graffiti was aimed, are not hopeful of catching those responsible.

There are also words, such as *means*, that are plural in form but can function as singular (even to the extent of being able to say *a means* or even *one means*) or plural depending on the words used with them:

(singular) *One means of identifying your dog is with an engraved disc.*
(plural) *Various means were employed to enrage the bull.*

Many nouns can be used as 'modifiers', like adjectives. On this role, see under **Knowing about adjectives**, p. 44.

Knowing about verbs

> *They've a temper, some of them [words] – particularly verbs: they're the proudest – adjectives you can do anything with, but not verbs.*
>
> Lewis Carroll, *Through the Looking Glass*, 1872

Verbs are words that describe an action (*get, walk, laugh, lie, spread, take*) or a state (*be, become, exist, remain*). They can refer in various ways, either on their own or with the help of another verb, to the present (*get, am walking, become*), to the past (*got, walked, became, have existed, have been walking, had remained*, etc.), or to the future (*will get, will walk, shall become, are going to arrive*). These differences in the time expressed by a verb are called **tenses**.

Who does what: subjects and objects
Verbs form the core of most sentences, round which the meaning is built. Each verb has a subject (the person or thing that is performing the action), and

some have an object (the person or thing affected by the action). If there is an object, the verb is called **transitive**:

subject	verb	object
Harry	*opened*	*the window.*

Compare this with:

subject	verb	object
The window	*opened.*	–

Here, the subject of the verb is *the window*, the verb is *opened*, and there is no object. In this case, the verb is called **intransitive**.

Some verbs can have two objects: a **direct object** (like 'the window' in the first example above) and what is called an **indirect object**. In the sentence *He gave the flowers to Susan*, 'to Susan' is the indirect object of the verb *gave*. You can also say *He gave Susan the flowers*, omitting the word *to*, and if you substitute a pronoun for this, you get the sequence *He gave her the flowers*, in which 'her' is the indirect object and 'the flowers' is the direct object:

subject	verb	indirect object	direct object
He	*gave*	*Susan* or *her*	*the flowers.*

Verbs that have two objects like this are sometimes called **ditransitive**. Verbs of giving are often ditransitive, and so are verbs of telling, asking, providing, and showing:

subject	verb	indirect object	direct object
I	*will tell*	*Charlie*	*what happened.*
He	*asked*	*me*	*a question.*
I	*will get*	*you*	*another cup.*
Molly	*showed*	*me*	*her room.*

You will find more about how to use verbs in effective ways to build sentences in the next section, **Building sentences**, p. 100.

Who you are talking about: number and person
Like nouns, verbs can be either **singular**, when they refer to one person or thing, or **plural**, when they refer to more than one. This is called **number**.

Verbs also have three **persons**, which are distinguished by their typical subjects:

person	refers to	subject	example
first	speaker(s)	*I, we*	*I love cake. We should be going.*
second	person or people addressed	*you*	*You are beautiful. Did you see that?*
third	some other person or people or things	*he, she, it, they,* or a noun	*David was here. She will see you now. The soldiers marched on. They have a lot to do.*

Verbs change their forms to denote which person (*I, you, he, they*, etc.) is meant and whether the action or state expressed by the verb is happening in the present, happened in the past, or will happen in the future. This process is called **inflection**. In the simple present, the only change to the verb is in the third person singular (after *he, she, it*, or a singular noun). The other main changes are the *-ing* form and the form *-ed* or *-t* in the past:

verb	third person singular	past	*-ing* form
blink	*blinks*	*blinked*	*blinking*
crunch	*crunches*	*crunched*	*crunching*
learn	*learns*	*learned* or *learnt*	*learning*
sit	*sits*	*sat*	*sitting*
think	*thinks*	*thought*	*thinking*

Some very common verbs, such as *be* and *have*, are irregular (*be* becomes *am* in the first person singular, *are* in the second person singular, and *is* in the third person singular; the plural forms are all *are*). Some verbs (like *sit* and *think* in the table) change their forms totally in the past, and this can cause occasional problems even to native speakers of English (e.g. many people use *sunk* for the past of *sink*, whereas the correct past form in modern English is *sank*).

Burned *or* burnt?

Some verbs of one syllable ending in *-l, -m, -n,* or *-p* (such as *burn* and *dream*) form a past tense and past participle ending in *-ed* or *-t*:

burn	burned	burnt
dream	dreamed	dreamt
dwell	dwelled	dwelt
lean	leaned	leant
leap	leaped	leapt
learn	learned	learnt
smell	smelled	smelt
spell	spelled	spelt
spill	spilled	spilt
spoil	spoiled	spoilt

Both forms are correct, but those in *-t* predominate when the participle is used as an attributive adjective (i.e. before a noun), e.g. *burnt cakes* and *spilt milk*. In important pieces of writing, take care to be consistent, because it can look untidy if you spell the same word differently in the same document.

When it all happens: choosing the right tense

Strictly speaking, English verbs have only two tenses, the present (*I am*) and past (*I was*). For some tenses we have to use other verbs, principally the verbs *be, do, have,* and *will,* to make the appropriate form of the verb: *We **were** waiting*; *You **do** complain a lot*; *I **shall*** *go*; *They will come*; *The French have joined the alliance*; *I knew I had seen her before*, and so on. These verbs have a 'helping' role and are called auxiliary verbs. The table below shows their main uses:

tense	verb used	example
present continuous	*be*	She **is reading** a book.
emphatic present	*do*	I **do enjoy** your visits.
future	*shall, will, be going to*	I **shall be** there tomorrow. **Will** you **be coming** too? They **are going to wait** behind.
future continuous	*shall* or *will be*	Sarah **will be coming** too.
emphatic past	*did*	We **did arrive** on time after all.
past continuous	*be*	They **were waiting** for three hours.
perfect	*have*	We **have seen** this film before.
perfect continuous	*have* or *has been*	Roger **has been looking** for you.
past perfect or pluperfect	*had*	When we met them they **had not eaten**.
future perfect	*shall have* or *will have*	By tomorrow they **will have read** my letter.

Choice of tense mostly corresponds to actual time, and the continuous tenses (*am going, were talking, has been looking*, etc., as distinct from *go, talked, has looked*, etc.) refer to action happening at the time of speaking or at the time referred to.

There are occasional exceptions to the correspondence of tense to time, mostly conventional uses such as the so-called 'historic present' used for dramatic effect in narratives (*Marie says nothing, and walks slowly to the window*) and the future used in polite requests (*Will that be all for now?*).

The **perfect** tense refers to action in the past in terms of the present, unlike the simple past which refers to a completed action in the context of its time. Compare:

*She **made** the dinner.* (relevant to the past)

and

*She **has made** the dinner.* (relevant to now: *come and get it!*)

The **past perfect** (or **pluperfect**) tense refers to action already completed at a time referred to in the past ('when we met them' in the example given in the table), and the **future perfect** tense refers to action that will be completed by a point referred to in the future ('tomorrow' in the example).

Do is used to form **emphatic** tenses, which imply a stronger rejection of their opposite than a simple form of the verb does: compare *I do enjoy your visits* (rejecting the idea of not enjoying them) with *I enjoy your visits* (a simple statement).

Choice of tense (called 'sequence of tenses') becomes more complex in reported speech, in which something a person has said is 'reported' by someone else: compare *I **want** to see him* with *She said she **wanted** to see him.* For more on this see the heading **Direct and indirect speech** in section 2, p. 128.

Shall and will

These two verbs have an important role. They are modal verbs – that is, they form 'moods' and tenses of other verbs. They can also form negatives and questions without needing the help of *do*, so you say *shall I?*, *will you?*, etc., and *I shall not.*

The main uses of *shall* and *will* are:

- to express a state or action in the future: *I shall tell you everything tomorrow.*
- to express an intention or instruction: *We will not tolerate such behaviour.*

There is often confusion about when to use *shall* and when to use *will*. In everyday speech, *shall* and *will* are normally contracted into the pronoun that comes before it (*I'll*, *you'll*, *she'll*, *they'll*, etc.) and then the distinction between the two forms becomes irrelevant. But there are occasions when you have to use the words in full, and then you have to make a choice:

- in more formal writing, when the contracted forms might appear too casual.
- in questions, when the order of verb and pronoun is reversed (*shall I?*, *will you?*, etc.).
- in negatives, when the contracted forms also differ between *shall* and *will* (*I shan't*, *you won't*, etc.).

Contracted forms of shall *and* will

This table shows the main shortenings of *shall* and *will*. Like all contracted verb forms, these should be used mainly in informal contexts, although they are becoming more common even in formal and official usage. The least satisfactory is *it'll*, which produces an awkward sound, and can grate even when being read silently.

I shall	**I'll**	*it shall*	**it'll**
I will	**I'll**	*it will*	**it'll**
you shall	**you'll**	*we shall*	**we'll**
you will	**you'll**	*we will*	**we'll**
he shall	**he'll**	*they shall*	**they'll**
he will	**he'll**	*they will*	**they'll**
she shall	**she'll**	*shall not*	**shan't**
she will	**she'll**	*will not*	**won't**

Traditionally in British English outside Scotland, *shall* is used in the first person (with *I* and *we*) to make simple statements relating to future time, and in questions to express a tentative suggestion or invitation:

(first person singular) *I **shall** have more to say about examinations in chapter 3.*
(first person plural) ***Shall** we talk about it over that cup of tea?*

Will is used to express future time in the second and third persons:

(second person singular and plural) *By doing this, you **will** enable us to claim back the tax you've already paid on your gift.*
(third person singular) *The Treasury has confirmed that VAT **will** not be imposed on books or newspapers.*
(third person plural) *What **will** they want to know about my home?*

To express an intention or instruction, the opposite applies: *will* is used in the first person, and *shall* in the second and third persons:

(first person) *I **will** never travel again in the front coach.* (Or, more informally: *I **won't** ever travel again in the front coach.*)
(second person) *'I must take advice,' said George. 'So you **shall**, my dear,' said his wife.*
(second person) *You **shall** (old form thou **shalt**) have no other gods before me.*
third person *All personnel brought on to the property **shall** be required to abide by the safety rules.*

These guidelines represent the traditional distinction between *shall* and *will*, but in practice *will* can be used in almost all cases, and *shall* is often found in the first person when there is a strong element of intention. This is partly because the meaning distinction – between simple future statements and statements of intention – is often blurred. So in the last group of three examples, *shall* could easily be substituted for *will* in the first example and *will* for *shall* in the second and third (✓ *I **shall** never travel again* . . . and ✓ *So you **will**, my dear*).

Shall is less versatile, however, and is not idiomatic in the second and third persons in statements and questions that deal with simple information rather than expressing intention or instruction (**✗** *What* **shall** *they want to know about my home?*).

Regional variation

In Scottish English, and also in the English of Ireland and America, it is normal practice to use *will* in all cases, even in the first person when in British English you would expect *shall*:

Will I help you with your bags?

Should and would
Like *shall* and *will*, *should* and *would* are modal verbs that can form negatives and questions without the help of *do* (*I should not* or *I shouldn't*; *would you?*; *would they not?* or *wouldn't they?*). They are used mainly:

• in past tenses, in place of *shall* and *will*:

I didn't realize Jenny **would** *be there.*

• to express a tentative wish or request:

I **should** *like to ask you something.*
Would *they like to come too?*

• in conditional *if*-clauses:

I **should** *be late if I didn't have the car.*
They **wouldn't** *mind if we waited a while.*

Traditionally, *should* and *would* have the same distinction in use that *shall* and *will* have when referring to future action, *should* being used with *I* and *we*, and *would* being used with the second and third persons. In practice, however, *would* is often used in all these cases.

This usage is complicated by the fact that *should* has special roles not shared by *would* but corresponding to meanings of *ought to* and *must*:

- to express obligation or advice:

*I **should** have taken you for a walk tonight.*
*You **should** get a little dog like ours.*
*Students **should** be encouraged to self-monitor.*

- to express probability:

*The dinner **should** be ready soon.*
*They **should** have reached Madrid by now.*

To avoid confusion with these meanings, it is usually better to use *would* and not *should* in the first person:

*I **would** have taken you for a walk if we'd had more time.*

For more on *should* in conditions, see *If*-clauses in section 2, p. 124.

Who does what: active and passive verbs
Verbs can be active or passive. This is called **voice**. In the active voice, the subject of the verb performs the action, as in *Henry wrote a book*. In the passive voice, the object of the action becomes the grammatical subject, and the performer of the action, if stated at all, is introduced by a preposition, normally *by*, as in *The book was written by Henry*.

Passive verbs are formed with the verb *be*, and other

verbs are used to form so-called 'semi-passives' in which the past participle of the verb is at least partly adjectival (e.g. *He got changed* and *They seem bothered*).

Using passive verbs can be an effective way of saying what you want to say, especially when the recipient of an action, rather than the performer, is the main point of a statement. But some uses of the passive have a stilted and awkward effect on writing. In more formal and official writing it has acquired a bad reputation as a tool used to achieve vagueness and obfuscation.

The following are especially notorious uses:

- impersonal constructions with *it*:

? *It is recommended that you take the action described in section 3 of the attached information sheet.*

This is a style regularly found in official documents and reports, when they seek to avoid the personal responsibility that is implied by the active voice (*We recommend that you take the action described in section 3 . . .*). But this style is not suitable for ordinary writing and speaking.

- a double passive:

? *The undertaking was attempted to be completed.*

This awkward construction occurs with verbs such as *attempt, begin, desire, endeavour, propose, threaten*, and others involving constructions with a passive infinitive. It should be avoided when there is no corresponding active form (**✗** *They attempted the undertaking to be completed*), and a fully active construction should be used instead:

✓ *They attempted to complete the undertaking.*

In some cases the sentence can be rephrased; for example:

✓ *There was an attempt to complete the undertaking.*

Other verbs, such as *expect, intend,* and *order,* which are grammatically more versatile, will allow a double passive construction. For example, we can say:

✓ *They ordered the offenders to be punished.*

and therefore a double passive form is allowed:

✓ *The offenders were ordered to be punished.*

Infinitives

Verbs have special forms that work as different parts of speech, principally nouns and adjectives but also occasionally as prepositions. These are called infinitives and participles.

The **infinitive** of a verb is the simple form that is used, for example, as the headword in a dictionary: *break, come, do, have, generate, mollify, pretend,* etc. as distinct from the inflected forms *breaks, broke, broken, had, mollified,* and so on that are used in sentences to correspond to different contexts. These inflected forms denote tense (present, past, future) and number (singular or plural) and are called **finite**. The infinitive does not specify any of these things and is 'non-finite': hence the name *infinitive*.

The simple or 'bare' infinitive is used with other auxiliary or 'helping' verbs to form certain tenses (*will break, should go,* etc., as we saw on p. 22).

Some other verbs, especially verbs expressing wish

or obligation, require the infinitive to have the word *to* (here called a **particle**) before it: *I want **to see**, We like **to walk**, There is no need **to shout**, It is wrong to **kill people**.* For convenience we can call this type a *to*-infinitive. That little word *to* can cause all sorts of trouble, as we shall see.

To err is human, to forgive divine

You can also use an infinitive with *to* as a verbal noun, as with *to err* and *to forgive* in the heading above, which could also be expressed in the form ***Erring** is human, **forgiving** is divine*. Choice between this and an *-ing* form is largely a matter of style and personal preference. In other cases, there is not always a choice. For example, you *hope **to do** something* but you *think **of doing** some-thing*, *have a liking **for doing** something*, and *have an aversion **to doing** something*. You need to be careful not to confuse these patterns, especially when more than one is used in the same sentence.

Split infinitives

> Tell him or her . . . that when I split an infinitive, God damn it, I split it so it will stay split.

Raymond Chandler in a letter of 1947 to the editor of *Atlantic Monthly*,
reacting to a copy-editor's correction of his English

A split infinitive occurs when you need a *to*-infinitive and a word or phrase comes between *to* and the verb:

*I tried **to really love** them.*
*The victorious army proceeded **to cruelly and brutally kill** and pillage.*

Infinitives have been split since Middle English (the form of English in use from the 12th century, after the Norman Conquest) but the practice was less popular from the 16th century to the end of the 18th. There are no split infinitives in Shakespeare. In the 19th century it came back into favour, and can be found in the work of well-known writers, such as Byron:

*To sit on rocks to muse o'er flood and fell, **To slowly trace** the forest's shady scene.*

Despite these shifts in usage, nobody objected to splitting a *to*-infinitive until relatively recently, and the term itself is not found until the end of the 19th century. Before that, no one bothered much about it, and there is no grammatical reason for always keeping the two parts of an infinitive together. The argument that *to* and the verb form a unit does not accord with other verb patterns in English. For example, we regularly separate a verb from an auxiliary verb in uses such as *I have never agreed* and *They are always complaining*.

But just because we may split an infinitive does not mean that we always should. The normal position for an adverb is often before or after it, not within it:

? *Everything seemed **to suddenly change**.*

The normal order is:

✓ *Everything suddenly seemed to change.*

The adverb can also come after the infinitive:

✓ *Everything seemed to change suddenly.*

However, there are cases where the adverb has to go immediately before the verb to make the meaning clear:

✓ *The local authority is seeking **to gradually increase** the use of its public libraries.*

Here, *gradually* and *increase* form a unified concept, and alternatives produce an awkward style and rhythm:

? *The local authority is seeking to increase gradually the use of its public libraries.*
? *The local authority is seeking gradually to increase the use of its public libraries.*

Avoiding a split infinitive can lead to results that are just as unnatural, often stylistically poor, and in some cases ambiguous or misleading:

? *The Education Secretary has set out proposals that attempt **radically to change** the way in which pupils apply for university places.* (*to change radically* would be better; but *to radically change* is the natural choice)
? *She used **secretly to admire** him.*

In these examples the adverbs have a close association with their verbs, and separating them blurs the meaning as well as producing a poor rhythm.

In some cases, the adverb becomes attached to the wrong verb:

✗ It was in Paris that the wartime alliance began **finally to break up**.

✗ Charlie started **quietly to sing** snatches from the songs.

In the first example, *finally* refers to the breaking up and not to the beginning. More seriously, in the second example, it is not clear whether Charlie started quietly or continued quietly.

When an intensifying adverb such as *actually, even, ever, further, just, quite, really* belongs with a verb that happens to be an infinitive, it is usually better (and sometimes necessary) to place it between *to* and the verb:

✓ You can't buy anything **to actually fit** a newborn baby.

✓ We're meeting next week **to really get** this show on the road.

✓ Peter still managed **to quite like** him.

✓ He'd never be able **to fully appreciate** how beautiful the place is.

In the first example, you could say *You can't actually buy anything to fit a newborn baby*, but the emphasis would be changed. In the last example, some people might insist on saying **?** *He'd never be able fully to appreciate how beautiful the place is*, but this is unnatural and unidiomatic. A more satisfactory alternative is:

✓ He'd never be able to appreciate fully how beautiful the place is.

There are two particular circumstances in which it is best to avoid a split infinitive, because the split is clumsy or awkward:

• when the part that comes between is a phrase:

✗ *You two shared a curious ability **to without actually saying anything make** me feel dirty.*

There is an exception to this, when words such as 'more than' come before the verb, forming a united concept like 'gradually increase' which we saw earlier:

✓ *Prices are likely **to more than double**.*

• when a negative or limiting word such as *not, never, scarcely*, goes with the infinitive:

✗ *I wanted **to never see him** again.*
✓ *I wanted never to see him again.*
✓ *I never wanted to see him again.*

> *Invention No. 951,000: The way to always keep your temper. Never – lose it. Keep it in a cage tied round your waist.*
>
> Frances Hodgson Burnett, *Racketty-Packetty House*, 1912

Participles

There are two kinds of participle, those typically ending in *-ing* (the present participle) and those typically ending in *-ed*, *-t*, or *-n* (the past participle). Their forms and functions are as follows, with past forms also included for completeness:

verb	present participle	past tense	past participle
talk	talking	talked	talked
run	running	ran	run
learn	learning	learned or learnt	learned or learnt
see	seeing	saw	seen

verb	present participle	past tense	past participle
take	taking	took	taken
be	being	was	been
go	going	went	gone
hit	hitting	hit	hit
make	making	made	made

• **present participles** are used to form the so-called 'continuous' tenses which describe an action going on, e.g. *she **is talking**, they **were running***. They also function as adjectives (modifiers), e.g. *the **walking** boy*, and as nouns, e.g. ***walking** is good for you; she is not used to **travelling***; *they went out without **closing** the door.*

• **past participles** are used to form the past tense with *have* (called the perfect tense, as in *I **have gone**, **has she seen** you?*) and also passive forms of verbs (as in *the books **were taken**, the message **was sent***).

Participles can be used very effectively to introduce subordinate clauses that are attached without too much fuss to other words in a sentence; for example:

*She offered him one of the apples, **holding** it out at arm's length, without a smile.*
***Clutching** his package tightly, he looked round to make sure there was no one who could overhear him.*
***Educated** at Eton and Oxford, he served with the Grenadier Guards in World War I.*

Participles in initial position, as in the last two examples, are acceptable grammatically but when over-done can produce a poor style, especially when the participial clause bears little relation to the main one:

? *Being elected to parliament in 1952, she devoted the last years of her life to writing.*

Dangling participles
Beware of so-called 'unattached', 'misrelated', or 'dangling' participles, when the participle does not refer to the noun to which it is grammatically attached, normally the subject of the sentence:

✗ *Regarded by rail inspectors as the biggest single danger on the network, 18 people were killed on crossings last year.*

Most people on reading this sentence will know what it means, but at first it can make you start. Grammatically, if not actually, the implication is that the victims were to blame for their own deaths, whereas the real danger lies, of course, with the crossings. Confusing the reader like this, even only momentarily, can never be right. The best way of dealing with this ambiguity is to avoid it altogether by rephrasing the sentence:

Crossings, on which 18 people were killed last year, are regarded by rail inspectors as the biggest single danger on the network.

or:

18 people were killed on crossings last year, and these are regarded by rail inspectors as the biggest single danger on the network.

Here are some rather doubtful examples of unattached participles:

? *Being* a vegan bisexual who's into Nicaraguan coffee picking and boiler suits, you could safely assume that I vote Labour.

? *Driving* near home recently, a thick pall of smoke turned out to be a bungalow well alight.

Although, as these examples show, unattached participles seldom cause real ambiguity, they can jar and distract the reader, and are best avoided.

Certain participles, such as *considering, assuming, excepting, given, provided, seeing, speaking* (*of*), etc., have virtually become prepositions or conjunctions in their own right, and their use in a grammatically free role is now standard:

Speaking of the high cost of living, don't think we've forgotten the poll tax.
A long journey might be inadvisable, **considering** her great age.
Given that prices have already been set and cannot be changed, what will happen to real output?
The meeting will be held in the autumn. **Assuming** we are still in business, of course.

Naming it and doing it: related nouns and verbs

Some words are used both as nouns and as verbs. In some cases there is no difference in form or pronunciation, whereas in others either the form or pronunciation changes, or both change. When the pronunciation changes, it is usually the stress (the part of the word that is spoken with greater emphasis): the noun is usually stressed on the first syllable and the verb on the second, as with *conduct, extract, progress, record,* and *transfer.*

noun	verb	change in form?	change in pronunciation?
cloth	clothe	yes	yes
colour	colour	no	no
conduct	conduct	no	yes
extract	extract	no	yes
half	halve	yes	yes
nibble	nibble	no	no
practice	practise	yes	no
progress	progress	no	yes
record	record	no	yes
review	review	no	no
score	score	no	no
transfer	transfer	no	yes
turn	turn	no	no

Some nouns have affected the pronunciation of their corresponding verbs, so that (for example) *decrease*, *import*, and *transfer* are increasingly heard with a stress on the first rather than the second syllable as verbs as well as nouns. More controversially, some nouns are now heard stressed on the first syllable in place of a traditional second-syllable stress in both the noun and the verb (e.g. *dispute* and *research*, the latter under American influence).

Turning ideas into actions: verbs from nouns

By a process called 'conversion', verbs have for several centuries been formed from nouns (and occasionally adjectives), by using the same word (e.g. *to question*, *to knife*, *to quiz*, *to service*), by adding a suffix such as

-*ize* (*prioritize, randomize*), or by a shortening of the noun in a process called 'back-formation' (*to diagnose* from *diagnosis*, to *televise* from *television*). Although objections are raised to some of these formations (especially the longer ones in -*ize*, such as *hospitalize* and *privatize*), it is an established process and generally a useful one. No one now objects to *authorize* or *realize*, which were formed in exactly the same way. The table below shows a selection of now common -*ize* verbs that have come into use over several centuries, some surprisingly early. Their earliest meanings are not, however, always those in use today.

agonize	16c	*glamorize*	20c
anglicize	18c	*harmonize*	15c
antagonize	17c	*hypnotize*	19c
apologize	16c	*idolize*	16c
authorize	12c–14c	*itemize*	19c
brutalize	18c	*legitimize*	18c
capitalize	18c	*maximize*	19c
categorize	18c	*modernize*	18c
centralize	19c	*monopolize*	17c
characterize	16c	*nationalize*	19c
civilize	17c	*organize*	12c–14c
colonize	17c	*patronize*	16c
criticize	17c	*penalize*	19c
demoralize	18c	*politicize*	18c
deputize	18c	*prioritize*	20c
economize	17c	*publicize*	20c
equalize	16c	*realize*	17c
familiarize	17c	*recognize*	12c–14c
fantasize	20c	*scrutinize*	17c

socialize	19c	*utilize*	19c
specialize	17c	*vandalize*	19c
stabilize	19c	*victimize*	19c
standardize	19c	*visualize*	19c
subsidize	18c	*vitalize*	17c

-ing *words: verbal nouns*

A **verbal noun** (also called a **gerund**) is a form of a verb ending in *-ing* that acts as a noun, for example *working* in the sentences *I like working* and *Working keeps the mind active*. It should be distinguished from verbal adjectives (or participial adjectives), which have a describing role like other adjectives (as in *a working mother*) and identical forms of verbs (called participles) that are used to form continuous tenses (as in *I was still working at nine*).

A verbal noun is a part of a verb as well as being a noun, and so it can behave like a verb grammatically. This means that you can say, for example, *They objected to my working* (with the possessive form *my*) or *They objected to me working* (non-possessive): both are well established in ordinary usage, although the first, in which *working* is treated as a full noun, is preferable in more formal writing.

There are some guidelines you can follow when choosing between these two alternatives.

You generally prefer a possessive form:

• when the word preceding the *-ing* form is a personal name or a noun denoting a person:

*She did not know what to think about **Jonathan's walking out** like that.*
*I was now counting on **my father's being able** to make some provision somehow.*

You generally use a non-possessive form:

• when the noun is non-personal or in the plural:

*We had another discussion about **the house being** redecorated.*
*They had forgotten about **their visitors arriving** that week.*

• with indefinite pronouns (e.g. *anyone, everyone, somebody*):

*He couldn't contemplate **anyone else taking on** the work.*
*There are good reasons for **everybody wanting** to take part.*

With personal pronouns, you can use either the possessive or the non-possessive, but the possessive is more common when it comes first in a sentence:

***Their being** so generous came as a complete surprise.* (But the problem could be avoided by rephrasing: *Their generosity came as a complete surprise* will do nicely.)
*Do you mind **my asking** what you did with the money?*
*Fancy **him losing** his temper like that.*

In any of these sentences, the alternative form could be substituted with little difference to the meaning and none to grammatical integrity.

Knowing about adjectives

The adjective is the banana peel of the parts of speech.

Clifton Fadiman, *Reader's Digest*, 1956

Adjectives are words that describe or classify nouns in various ways, e.g. *red, large, pleasant, young, tiny, square, wooden, military, weekly*. The first five of these adjectives, up to *tiny*, are all used to describe people and things in ways that can vary and are not essential to their nature. These are called **descriptive** adjectives. The rest, from *square* to *weekly*, classify what they describe: that is to say, they identify an essential characteristic that is by its nature invariable. One thing can be larger or more or less pleasant than another, but an object is either wooden or it isn't. Other **classifying** adjectives include the nationality adjectives such as *English, French, Egyptian*, and *Japanese*.

Adjectives are also classed according to their position in the sentence. They can stand before the noun they describe (or classify), e.g. *a red car, a German sausage*. This is called the **attributive** position (because the adjective is regarded as an 'attribute' of the noun). Or they can come after a linking verb such as *be, become, look, seem*, etc., e.g. *the car is red, his face looked sad, her mother is German*. This is called the **predicative** position (because it comes in the predicate of the sentence: see section 2, p. 101).

Most adjectives can be used in either position without any change in meaning, but some can only be used in attributive position (before a noun), e.g. *elder*, and others can only be used in predicative position, e.g. *afraid, awake, alive, glad*: you can say *the girl was awake* but not *the awake girl*, and you can say *the people are glad* but not *the glad people*. Many more technical classifying adjectives are used mainly in the attributive position (e.g. *atomic, cardiac, subterranean*).

Adjectives that are used for emphasis, such as *absolute*, *entire*, *total*, and *utter*, are normally used only in the attributive position: *an absolute shame, the entire week, a total failure, an utter disaster*. Some of these work in predicative position, but the meaning changes somewhat. You can say *a total failure* or *their failure was total* (but this is less natural and a little unusual), and the same is true of *absolute* though not of *entire* or *utter*.

A few adjectives change their meaning when they change their position; or, to put it another way, they have different meanings with different restrictions. A good example is the adjective *late*. In its main meaning ('after the due or expected time') it is normally predicative. If you say *the team is late*, you mean the time has past when you expected the team to arrive, whereas *the late team* would mean the team that no longer exists, or whose members have all died.

A few adjectives are put immediately after the noun they are qualifying, e.g. *president elect, riches galore, the devil incarnate*. These are called **postpositive**. An adjective is also postpositive in a use such as *we must find the people responsible* (in which a link such as 'who are' can be understood between *people* and *responsible*).

Instead of *adjective*, some linguists prefer the term **modifier**, which includes words that are traditionally described as adjectives, and also words like *coffee* in *coffee table*, where *coffee* is describing (or modifying) the word *table* in much the same way as *low* or *wooden* might be but is traditionally classed as a noun (which it is normally, e.g. in a phrase like *have some coffee*). So 'modifiers' can be adjectives and also nouns when they are used like adjectives.

Types and order of adjectives

Most native speakers of English use adjectives intuitively, but knowing about the underlying pattern of use can help you to use them more effectively. Descriptive or 'qualitative' adjectives (describing size, age, quality, etc., such as *old, dark, deep, lovely*) come first, then colour adjectives (if any) and finally a classifying adjective (or noun used as a modifier). If there is a possessive word such as *my* or *his*, this comes first:

tall blue wild flowers
his old green outdoor coat
their wonderful recent French holiday

When to use commas

Note also that when you have a string of adjectives they are not normally separated by commas if they are of different types:

a large black cat
an old French woman

But when the adjectives are describing the same sort of thing, they are normally separated by commas. This practice has the effect of emphasizing each adjective more, because it introduces a slight pause before the next adjective, and it adds force to writing:

a cold, windy morning
a beautiful, soft voice

More *and* most: *comparatives and superlatives*

Descriptive adjectives have three forms, traditionally called a positive (or absolute), e.g. *hot, splendid*, a comparative, e.g. *hotter, more splendid*, and a superlative, e.g. *hottest, most splendid*.

These adjectives are sometimes described as gradable, because they can vary in intensity; you can say one thing is *larger* (or *more pleasant*) than another, and you can say one is *largest* (or *most pleasant*). *Larger* and *more pleasant* are called the comparative forms, and *largest* and *most pleasant* are called the superlative forms of the adjectives *large* and *pleasant*.

Adjectives of one syllable and some adjectives of two syllables form their comparative and superlative forms by adding *-er* and *-est*, sometimes with a change of the stem (*soft, softer, softest; able, abler, ablest; common, commoner, commonest; happy, happier, happiest*). Note that adjectives of two syllables ending in *-le* and *-y* usually have forms in *-er* and *-est*: others are *nobler, noblest; suppler, supplest; fruitier, fruitiest; smokier, smokiest*. Some other two-syllable adjectives also have these forms, but these are less predictable and do not follow a clear rule: the ones in most frequent use are *common* and *pleasant*. If you are unsure in a particular case, you should check in a good dictionary that includes information about how words change their forms.

Other adjectives of two syllables, and all adjectives of more than two, normally make their comparative and superlative forms by adding *more* or *most* instead of changing their form (*more honest, more peaceful, most frightening, most remarkable*).

These comparative and superlative forms of adjectives are used in particular ways:

• The comparative form is used with *than* to compare two people or things (or facts and possibilities, as in the second example below), or without *than* to compare one state with another state that is implied but not expressed:

*The site operators enforce safety controls far **tougher than** those insisted on by Government.*
*She wasn't staying in this building one instant **longer than** she had to.*
*They were **happier** in the country watching birds.*
*It is a false economy to buy a **milder**, **cheaper** Cheddar for cooking.*

• The superlative form is used to indicate an extreme among three or more (or a vague or undefined number of) people or things or possibilities:

*He was the **happiest** man alive.*
*They were **best** when they were not rushed.*

Special effects

For a special purpose, often to make a jocular or ironic point, an adjective of several syllables will sometimes be inflected:

'Curiouser and curiouser!' cried Alice.
Important? It was the importantest thing he had ever done.

Conversely, *more* and *most* are sometimes used, for emphasis or special effect, when inflected forms are available (*truer* and *nobler* in these examples):

> *We could relate to one another in a more true fashion.*
> *There is nothing more noble than a mature pine forest.*

Some adjectives have an all-or-nothing kind of meaning and cannot be qualified by *more* or *most*. These are called **absolute** or **non-gradable** adjectives. The table below shows the difference between gradable and non-gradable adjectives. Those in the left-hand column can vary in force or intensity, whereas those in the right-hand column are absolutes and cannot vary (and many of these are classifying adjectives such as *rectangular*, *Dutch*, and *weekly*:

gradable	non-gradable
happy	dead
long	rectangular
difficult	Dutch
hungry	female
absurd	manual
trivial	weekly

Non-gradable adjectives are not normally used in comparative or superlative forms and cannot be qualified by adverbs that intensify or moderate such as *fairly*, *largely*, *more*, *rather*, or *very*.

There are exceptions to this rule, when a non-gradable adjective is used in a special way that makes it effectively gradable for the moment:

All animals are equal but some animals are more equal than others.
Her sister is very Italian. (= has a strong Italian character)

However, non-gradable adjectives can be qualified by adverbs that denote a complete or extreme state, such as *absolutely*, *completely*, and *utterly*:

✓ *The Greeks are absolutely fearless.*
✓ *She still found it all utterly unbelievable.*

In this sentence, *absolutely fearless* is acceptable, and so is *completely* or *utterly fearless*, but *fairly* or *rather fearless* is logically much less plausible, except in casual conversation.

Than I *or* than me?

? *Frank is more serious about it than I.*
? *Frank is more serious about it than me.*

You may be unsure which form of a pronoun to use after *than*, when it stands alone: *I* or *me*, *he* or *him*, *she* or *her*, *we* or *us*, *they* or *them*. (The problem obviously does not arise with *you* or *it*, nor with nouns, which do not change their form in the same way.)

The answer is that both forms are permissible, because *than* can operate as a preposition or as a conjunction. If you say:

Frank is more serious about it than I

you are using *than* as a conjunction, and the verb *am* is understood. You are effectively saying:

Frank is more serious about it than I am.

(And you can get round the problem altogether by using this full form.)

If you say:

Frank is more serious about it than me

you are using *than* as a preposition, which like all prepositions takes the objective form of pronouns (e.g. *me*, *him*, *her*, *us*, and *them*).

For more on pronouns, see **Knowing about pronouns**, p. 62.

Wrong use of the superlative

Comparative and superlative forms can also be used with the determiner *the* to denote which of a group has the more (in the case of two) or most (in the case of more than two) of the quality being described:

*We divided the work into two sections and I took the **longer**.*
*Which of the children is the **tallest**?*

It is generally considered incorrect to use the superlative form when you are only talking about two people or things:

✗ *We divided the work into two sections and I took the longest.*

There are some exceptions, mostly in familiar set expressions:

*Mother knows **best**.*
*Put your **best** foot forward.*

Knowing about adverbs

> *I'm glad you like adverbs – I adore them; they are the*
> *only qualification I really much respect.*
>
> Henry James, in a letter of 1912

Types of adverb

Adverbs form a wide range of words that behave very differently from each other but basically describe how, why, when, how often, or where something happens or is done:

type	answers question	examples
adverbs of manner	how?	*slowly, unpleasantly, separately*
adverbs of time	when?	*tomorrow*
adverbs of frequency	how often?	*often, never, usually, weekly*
adverbs of place	where?	*upstairs, abroad, in the garden*
adverbs of distance	how far?	*all the way, to the end of the road*
adverbs of degree	to what extent?	*very, slightly, definitely*

Adverbs can be single words or phrases; if they are phrases (e.g. *in the garden, all the way*) they are sometimes called **adverbials**. They can qualify verbs (*They walked **slowly***), adjectives (*an **unpleasantly** gruff man*), other adverbs (*She took it **very** well*), or even whole sentences (see **Sentence adverbs**, p. 61).

How adverbs are formed
Adverbs are formed in the following main ways:

• Most adverbs are formed by adding *-ly* to adjectives (with a further change of spelling in some words, such as *happy*):

candid	*candidly*
quick	*quickly*
happy	*happily*
capable	*capably*

• Some adjectives do not form adverbs in this way, although we might expect them to: for example, the adverb from *fast* is not *fastly*, but *fast*, and the adverb from *straight* is not *straightly* but *straight*. The adjectives *hard* and *late*, and some others, form adverbs *hardly* and *lately* only in special senses (otherwise the adverbs are the same as the adjectives):

hard	*He hit the ball **hard**.*	*She **hardly** knew what to say.*
high	*The balloon rose **high**.*	*That was **highly** dangerous.*
late	*We arrived **late**.*	*Kim has been looking tired **lately**.*
right	*I hope I've done it **right**.*	*They were **rightly** criticized.*

• Some words ending in *-ly* and denoting frequency are adjectives as well as adverbs: e.g. *daily, hourly, monthly, weekly, yearly*:

(adverb) *The lavatories are cleaned **hourly**.*
(adjective) *The bus company operates an **hourly** service.*

• In other cases, adjectives are used as adverbs only informally, often in fixed expressions such as *come clean* and *hold tight*. To these we can add *real* and *sure*, which are characteristic of informal American speech (*That was real nice* and *I sure liked seeing you*) and are also found in non-standard and dialect use in Britain.

Comparatives and superlatives

Like adjectives, some adverbs are gradable and can form comparative and superlative forms in *-er* and *-est*, or by using *more* and *most*: *fast, faster, fastest*; *funny, funnier, funniest*; *happily, more happily, most happily*.

Adverbs of degree

Adverbs of degree divide into four types that all have a special role: they are called emphasizing adverbs, intensifying adverbs, moderating adverbs, and focussing adverbs:

• emphasizing adverbs include *certainly, definitely, literally, really, simply*:

*This was **certainly** the only man she had ever held in her arms.*
*We had a good time and will **definitely** come again.*
*It **really** hurts me to be going away.*

• intensifying adverbs include *very, extremely, greatly, immensely*:

*He was **very** funny, and lots of women found him attractive.*
*She feels **extremely** frustrated and isolated.*
*Darrel was already **deeply** in debt.*

• moderating adverbs include *fairly, pretty, quite, rather, slightly, somewhat*:

*Danielle had natural ability and a **rather** pushy mother.*
*She felt cold and **slightly** sick.*
*In the following two weeks tensions eased **somewhat**.*

• focussing adverbs include *even, just, merely, only, purely, simply*:

*It was a long time before I could **even** change her nappy.*
*If you'll excuse me I'll **just** take a little nap.*
*The first problem was **simply** a lack of data.*

Use of time words as adverbs

The adverbial use of days of the week (singular and plural) and similar words is a common feature of American English and also occurs in informal British English:

***Tuesday night**, the board approved the addition of a new subsection.*
*I was to be offered an option of taking her with me **summers**.*

These uses are not normally acceptable in Standard British English, and would almost certainly be frowned on if encountered in more formal types of writing.

Where adverbs go

The position of adverbs in phrases and clauses follows fairly definite patterns. There are three basic positions: at the beginning of a sentence (called **initial position**), in the middle of a sentence (called **mid position**) and at the end of a sentence (called **end position**).

These are a few examples of the most common positions, but there are others that native speakers know instinctively:

• In simple statements, they can come between the subject and its verb when the verb is followed by an object or other continuation:

*Scotland, France's ally, **dutifully** declared war on England.*
*They **suddenly** found the room, at the end of a long corridor.*
*Hardy **gradually** excluded Emma from his professional life.*
*The truth **eventually** dawned on them.*

• This applies in particular to intensifying and frequency adverbs such as *even*, *often*, *only*, and *usually*:

*These days, you **even** get your own room.*
*We **usually** meet on a Friday.*

• When there is an auxiliary verb, an adverb typically comes between this and the main verb:

*The crystal glasses have to be **carefully** washed by hand.*
*Keep track of your location so that the glider does not **inadvertently** stray into controlled airspace.*
*They had **often** met secretly.*
*He had **accidentally** set fire to his room by knocking over a lighted candle.*

• For special emphasis, or when the adverb belongs closely to what follows the main verb, it can come in a position that differs from these rules, for example after the verb or before it, or in initial or end position:

*Be sure you **really** can do what you claim.* (With emphasis on *can*; normal order would be *be sure you can really do . . .*)
*The children listened **carefully**, and tried hard to understand.*
***Gradually** replies filtered back to him.*
*The intention is to set each subject **briefly** in context.*
*He needed to try **harder**.*

• An intensifying or moderating adverb typically goes with the adjective or other word it refers to:

*We had **really** good teachers from the local St John Ambulance Brigade.*
*Eating should be a pleasure and not **merely** a means of fuelling the body.*

• Adverbs of time and place, and most adverb phrases (consisting of more than one word), often come at the beginning or end of the sentence:

*Official negotiations were still in progress **yesterday**.*
***In the garden** there stood a huge walnut tree.*
*Maths explains things very well, **up to a point**.*

Where to put *only*

The position of the little word *only* in a sentence causes special problems when it is used as an adverb. Its natural position is not always the same as the logical position, and this has given rise to the superstition that the logical position should always take precedence.

The logical position is close to the word it refers to, but the natural position is usually between the subject and its verb:

(natural position) *I can **only** lend you five pounds.*
(logical position) *I can lend you **only** five pounds.*

The first sentence shows the natural or idiomatic position of *only*, and the second sentence shows the logical but unidiomatic position. Strictly speaking, the first sentence could be understood in a different way: not as meaning 'I can lend you five pounds but no more' (which is the obvious meaning) but 'I cannot give you five pounds but I can lend it'. Casting the sentence in the second way makes it clear, if necessary, that you have the first meaning in mind and not the second.

In its natural position between the subject and the verb, *only* can refer forward to different parts of longer statements:

✓ *He has **only** removed the part that was faulty.*
✓ *We **only** eat fish on Friday.*

In these cases, the word *only* would normally be understood as referring forward to 'the part that was faulty' and 'on Friday', i.e. 'he removed the faulty part but nothing else' and 'we eat fish on Friday but on no other day'. But each sentence has another possible meaning: 'he removed the faulty part but did not replace it' and 'on Friday we eat fish and nothing else'.

In speech, your tone of voice usually makes it clear what you mean. In written English, if you want to make it absolutely clear that you mean one thing and not the other, you can put the words in a different order:

(first meaning) ✓ *The **only** part he has removed is the part that was faulty.*
(second meaning) ✓ *The **only** thing he has done with the part that was faulty is to remove it.*
(first meaning) ✓ *It is **only** on Friday that we eat fish.*
(second meaning) **?** *On Friday we eat **only** fish.*

Note that in the last example a better style would be:

✓ *On Friday we **only** eat fish.*

This is open to the theoretical misunderstanding that 'we eat fish but don't do anything else with it'. But common sense tells us that the statement is not likely to be understood in this way. So the natural position of *only*, between *we* and *eat*, is preferable here.

Remember that you can often get round the problem by rephrasing the sentence when it becomes problematic, for example:

✓ *All he has done is remove the faulty part.*
✓ *Fish is all we eat on Friday.*

The logical position is used for greater emphasis, especially in formal contexts:

✓ *The time had come for him to be totally unselfish and think **only** of Anna.*
✓ *Peace will be possible **only** if it is guaranteed by an effective network of alliances.*
✓ *The tax is imposed **only** on income exceeding three times the average net personal income per worker.*

The superstition comes in when people insist on always putting *only* in its logical position. Normally, as with all moderating adverbs, it occurs idiomatically at an earlier point in the sentence:

✓ I **only** *know what I read in the papers.*
✓ *State support will* **only** *be provided for invalids and the elderly.*

How, where, *and* when
These are three busy words that are used to ask questions about manner, place, and time:

How *did you do that?*
Where *is she?*
When *are you going?*

They are also used to introduce relative clauses with the meanings 'in what way' or 'in which place' or 'at which time':

He wondered **how** *he could tell her.*
Tell me **where** *you have been.*
I don't know **when** *they will arrive.*

Where is sometimes used loosely in place of *in which*:

They may see a situation where [= in which] *they are not getting enough protection.*

This use is casual in tone and it is better to use *in which* in more formal or official contexts.

Wherever, whenever, however
Wherever and *whenever* should be written as one word when they are used as conjunctions introducing a clause:

They are going to have problems, **wherever** *they go.*

*She went off by train to **wherever** it is she's gone.*
*You can use our pool **whenever** you want.*
***Whenever** the soldiers saw us, they spat at us.*
*Local authorities should provide day classes **wherever** possible.*

In the last sentence, there is an ellipsis (omission) of *it is*, the full sense being 'wherever it is possible'.

But write *where ever* and *when ever* as two words when *where* or *when* is asking a question and *ever* has an intensifying role:

***Where ever** did you take them?*
***When ever** did you have the time?*

However is written as one word in its contrasting meaning 'on the other hand' and when it means 'in whatever way' or 'to whatever extent':

***However** you do it, do it quickly.*
***However** many women he took to himself, they were not Beth.*
*I don't think a respectable firm should take such a direction, **however** lucrative.*
*Tree shrews are, **however**, distinguished from squirrels by their long, pointed noses.*
***However**, the coastline has altered drastically in the last ten thousand years.*

It is written as two words when *how* is asking a question intensified by *ever*, in the same way as *where ever* and *when ever*. A sure way of identifying this meaning is to see if you can substitute *how on earth* for *how ever*: if you can, as in the example below, you spell it as two words:

How ever was he was going to tell her?
How ever did these get to Peru?

For more about *however*, see p. 259.

Sentence adverbs

Some adverbs (mostly ending in *-ly*, such as *clearly, frankly, happily, hopefully, personally, sadly, thankfully, unfortunately*) refer to a whole statement, and form a comment associated more closely with the speaker or writer than with what is said. In this role they are called 'sentence adverbs'. This use can be seen by comparing the use of *unhappily* as an ordinary adverb of manner (*She went unhappily to bed*) with its use as a sentence adverb (*She was, unhappily, too ill to leave the house*). In this use, the adverb often stands in initial position:

Frankly, it would be a relief to have something else to think about.
Sadly the congregation rarely has more than 15 worshippers.
Unfortunately, I was on the other side of the river when I saw him.

Sentence adverbs can also come in mid or end position:

The children clearly liked her.
After a long discussion, we were unfortunately refused.
They soon left, luckily.

Thankfully *and* hopefully

Use of sentence adverbs is well established in English, and the only ones that have given rise to controversy are *thankfully* and (in particular) *hopefully*:

? *A good system needs to be able to detect errors, and hopefully also to be able to employ some means of correcting them.*

? *Thankfully one thing we're not short of in this family is money.*

The reason for this seems to be that *thankfully* and *hopefully* cannot be resolved into an equivalent phrase in the way the others can (e.g. *clearly*: 'as is clear' and *sadly*: 'as is sad') but only into 'as is to be hoped'. But this objection is highly contrived and artificial, and some of the other sentence adverbs can only be resolved in this way with some awkwardness (*frankly*: 'as is frank'?).

Even so, the current state of play with *hopefully* is that it is best reserved for spoken use, and should be avoided in more formal writing, if only to avoid causing irritation to language purists who might be reading.

Knowing about pronouns

Who would succeed in the world should be wise in the use of his pronouns.

John Hay, *Distichs*, 1870s

A pronoun is a word such as *I, me, you, he, she, it, they, them, ourselves, this, those,* and so on, which refers to a person or thing already known. Pronouns are used to avoid repeating the nouns all the time (as you would have to in a sentence such as *Jennifer said that Jennifer would arrive tomorrow*).

The table below lists the different types of pronouns, with examples:

personal pronouns	*I (me), you, he (him), she (her), it, we (us), they (them)*
possessive pronouns	*mine, hers, his, its, yours, theirs*
demonstrative pronouns	*this, that, these, those*
relative pronouns	*what, who (whom), which, that, whose*
interrogative pronouns	*what, who, whom, which, whose*
indefinite pronouns	*anything, anyone, anybody, something, someone, somebody, everything, everyone, everybody*
reflexive pronouns	*myself, yourself, himself, herself, itself, oneself; ourselves, yourselves, themselves*
reciprocal pronouns	*each other, one another*

Personal pronouns
In the first and third persons, the personal pronouns have different forms for subjective and objective uses:

person	subjective	objective
first person singular	*I*	*me*
second person singular	*you*	*you*
third person singular	*he, she, it*	*him, her, it*
first person plural	*we*	*us*
second person plural	*you*	*you*
third person plural	*they*	*them*

The subjective form is used when the pronoun is the subject of a verb, and the objective form is used when it is the object (direct or indirect) of a verb or is governed by a preposition such as *on* or *to*:

***I** wish **I** could come.*
***She** will be here soon.*
*Helen phoned **me**.*
*Give **them** to **him**.*
*I saw **her** yesterday.*
*Tell **us** what Charles said.*

Between you and I, and similar mistakes
✗ *She doesn't mind. In fact, **between you and I** [✓ me], I think she's relieved.*
✗ *The messages passing **between Karen and he** [✓ him] were more complex.*

In the first sentence, *me* and not *I* is the correct form, and in the second sentence *him* and not *he*, since *between* governs both *you* and *me* in the first and both *Karen* and *him* in the second. *I* and *he* are the forms used for the subject of a sentence. The same applies to other prepositions used in this way (such as *at* and *for*):

✗ *The children were looking at Judith and I [✓ me].*

You can see this more clearly if you take out the first part of the object:

✗ *The children were looking at I.*
✓ *The children were looking at me.*

The mistake is now obvious.

After the verb *be* you can use both the subjective form of the pronoun (*I*, *we*, etc.) and the objective form (*me*, *us*, etc.); the objective forms are more natural and usual in ordinary spoken English:

*She said it was only **her**.*
*That's **them** standing by the door.*
*Is it **me** you wanted to see?*

The subjective forms can sound affected and unidiomatic, especially when they are repeated in the same sentence or when the first-person forms *I* and *we* are involved:

? *She said it was only **she**.*
? *That's **we** sitting on the bench.*

The more natural and idiomatic way of expressing these is:

✓ *She said it was only her.*
✓ *That's us sitting on the bench.*

The choice is more difficult when a relative clause (introduced by *who* or *that*) follows:

? *It was me who said it.*
✓ *It was I who said it.*

✓ *It was me that said it.*

He or she and alternatives
You may sometimes be unsure about what personal pronoun or possessive word (*his*, *her*, etc.) to put in sentences like the following:

*Anyone can feel free to say whatever **he/she/they** like.*
*Every candidate should submit **his/her/their** nomination papers by the end of the month.*

Here, *anyone* and *every* can stand for a male or female person with correspondingly different forms of possessive word. The safest and most widely accepted option is to put *he or she*, or *his or her*:

*Anyone can feel free to say whatever **he or she** likes.*
*Every candidate should submit **his or her** nomination papers by the end of the month.*

But this can be awkward, especially when the sentence continues for some time with repeated references back to the original subject. In cases like this it is now acceptable to use a plural form of pronoun to refer back to an indefinite pronoun, so as to avoid having to specify gender at all when this is unknown or irrelevant:

*Anyone can feel free to say whatever **they** like.*
*Every candidate should submit **their** nomination papers by the end of the month.*

This is a great deal neater, and is supported historically: the use of *they* and *their* in this way used to be common in English until people took against it in the 19th century, when other grammatical superstitions also arose (including objection to the split infinitive). But there is an alternative that gets round the problem altogether, by putting the whole sentence in the plural:

*People can feel free to say whatever **they** like.*
*All candidates should submit **their** nomination papers by the end of the month.*

The following sentence, taken from a newspaper, is couched in the singular for special effect, but it becomes more and more ungainly as it goes along:

? *The atheist requires as much faith to stand by their belief as the Christian does for theirs.*

The problem is solved, or rather avoided, by putting the whole sentence in the plural. Little of the individual effect is lost, and a big improvement in style is achieved:

✓ *Atheists require as much faith to stand by their belief as Christians do for theirs.*

This option is worth remembering, but you have to keep the sentence in the singular when you use singular indefinite pronouns such as *anyone* or *somebody*:

✓ *Does anyone want their tea now?*

And some plural sentences would result in even greater awkwardness or loss of meaning:

✓ *Each parent has a duty to do the best for their own child.*
? *All parents have a duty to do the best for their own children.*

When the sentence continues with repeated references back, attempts to maintain the gender distinction can become ridiculous. In the sentence about grammar that occurs in the preface to this book, such a problem arose. This is what I wrote:

In fact everyone knows a great deal more than they realize about the grammar of the language they speak as their mother tongue.

I much prefer this to any attempt to be artificially purist, which produces results that are at best ungainly and at worst absurd:

In fact everyone knows a great deal more than he or she realizes about the grammar of the language he or she speaks as his or her mother tongue.

I could have recast the sentence in the plural, but this would have altered the focus because I wanted to address the reader individually:

In fact people know a great deal more than they realize about the grammar of the language they speak as their mother tongue.

Mine and my, yours and your: possessive pronouns and determiners

You may not be familiar with the term **determiner**. Determiners stand before nouns and help to identify them in various ways, like the ones in the table below. For more about these see the end of this section, p. 97.

person	pronoun	determiner
first person singular	*mine*	*my*
second person singular	*yours*	*your*
third person singular	*hers, his, its, one's*	*her, his, its, one's*
first person plural	*ours*	*our*

person	pronoun	determiner
second person plural	*yours*	*your*
third person plural	*theirs*	*their*

The only one of these words to have an apostrophe is *one's*. This is because *one* is not strictly speaking a pronoun at all but a noun, and so it forms its possessive like other nouns, e.g. *the piano's tone, Valerie's room*.

These words are used to show who or what possesses something or who something relates to. They can all refer to one person or thing or to several:

*She looked great with a pierced nose so I had **mine** done too.*
*The experiences described in the book were **theirs** and not **hers**.*

The pronouns are also used with a preceding *of* to denote ownership in a more emphatic way and to allow another determiner (in this case, *this*) to be used:

*He will deliberately wreck this scheme **of ours**.*

Its *and* it's

Take special care to avoid misspelling the possessive *its* with an apostrophe, which is a common mistake. It is also a serious mistake because many people regard it as a sure sign of illiteracy. *It's* is not a possessive form at all but is a contraction of *it is* or *it has*:

✓ *It's* [= it is] *cold outside, and it's* [= it has] *been raining.*
✗ *The cat licked it's paws.*
✓ *The cat licked its paws.*

Other pronouns – that is, apart from the personal and possessive pronouns which we reviewed above – can also be determiners, i.e. can stand before nouns. For example, in the sentence *This is the house I lived in*, *this* is a pronoun because it stands alone. In the sentence *I lived in this house*, *this* is a determiner because it does not stand alone but qualifies the noun *house*. All the demonstrative pronouns can also be determiners, and so can the relative pronouns *which* and *whose* (but not *who* or *that*), and the interrogative pronouns *what*, *which*, and *whose* (but not *who* or *whom*).

This and *that*: *demonstrative pronouns, determiners, and adverbs*

| **singular** | *this* | *that* |
| **plural** | *these* | *those* |

This and *that*
As **pronouns**, *this* and *that* are used to specify a person or thing already mentioned. In general, *that* refers to a person, thing, or notion that is more remote or less familiar, whereas *this* refers to a person or thing either in the speaker's presence or under close or recent consideration:

That is not what most people come for at all.
This might be the one we want.

This and *that* can also refer to facts and statements expressed earlier in the sentence:

He has more children than I do and I am immensely jealous of
that.

The plural forms *these* and *those* have the same general
(and often vague) distinction:

*Could you take **these** as well?*
***Those** were the ones we decided to leave behind.*

As **determiners**, *this* and *that* qualify nouns:

*I found **this** book immensely valuable.*
*He was determined not to let **that** mistake happen again.*
***These** concerns were not shared by Mrs Thatcher.*
*In **those** days it was common for industrialists to go to the*
United States to learn how to run companies.

As **adverbs**, *this* and *that* have roles indicating extent
or degree:

*We can never be **this** good again.*
*I'm foolish going along with you even **this** far.*
*He didn't want to wait **that** long.*

These and those
Choice between the plural forms *these* and *those* corresponds to that between *this* and *that*, *these* implying
familiarity and closeness and those implying remoteness. *Those* also has a special identifying role followed
by a relative clause introduced by *that* or *who* (though
not normally by *which*) or *where* (equivalent to 'in
which' or 'at which'):

*I must draw attention to **those** places **that** have given me*
special pleasure.

Those candidates *who* recognize that they are unsuitable are able to drop out of the programme.

In *those* regions *where* rainfall is adequate, the soil tends to be poor.

The builders are involved in the project only at *those* stages *where* [= at which] they have special expertise.

It's one of *those* jobs *where* [= in which] the pay doesn't actually cover the cost of the lifestyle.

This construction is also found, though less often, with *when*:

He always took full advantage of *those* moments *when* Buddie showed an interest in him.

In *those* days *when* civilian travel was frowned upon we had no uniform to prove that our journey was really necessary.

Wh- words: relative pronouns and determiners

	things	person or people	person or people, thing or things	referring forward
singular and plural	*which*	*who* (*whom*)	*that*	*what*
possessive	*whose*	*whose*		
antecedent?	yes	yes	yes	no

These words – all beginning with *wh-* except for *that* – are used to introduce clauses that give more information about a person or thing that has been mentioned. They are used mostly as pronouns, i.e. they stand alone, like *who* in the first of the following examples and *which* in the second; but the possessive word *whose* when used in relative clauses is a determiner, i.e. it goes with a noun (*grounds* in the third sentence):

*Is he the man **who** spoke to you?*
*The writer tries to explore some of the factors **which** influence our disposition to commit crimes.*
*The local citizens through **whose** grounds the river flows are sensitive to pollution from the company.*
*Is this **what** you want?*

In the first two sentences, *who* and *which* refer back to the words 'the man' and 'the factors': these are called the **antecedents**. Notice that *what you want* is a kind of noun clause: *what* looks forward to the words that follow, and therefore does not have an antecedent, except in illiterate speech:

✗ *Is he the man **what** [✓ who or that] spoke to you?*

Who or whom?
    A certain young man never knew
    Just when to say *whom* and when *who*;
    'The question of choosing,'
    He said, 'is confusing;
    I wonder if *which* wouldn't do?'

Christopher Morley, Mince Pie, 1919

*It was not clear **who** had killed **whom**.*
*She knew nothing of his private life or **who** his friends were.*
***Whom** should we support in the elections?*
*For **whom** did you write these poems?*

Who is used as a relative pronoun (*the man who spoke to you*) and as an interrogative (in questions; *who spoke to you?*). *Whom* is the objective form of *who*, used as the object of verbs and prepositions (*the woman whom I met; the man to whom I spoke; Whom did you see?*).

In practice, especially in everyday English, *whom* is disappearing:

- In questions it is simply giving way to *who*: *Who did you see?*
- In relative clauses it is usually either replaced by *that* or omitted altogether: *the woman that I met* or *the woman I met* (*the woman who I met* still sounds awkward and is not generally acceptable).
- With prepositions, the normal usage is to omit *who* (or *that*) and place the preposition at the end: *the woman I spoke to*. By contrast, putting a preposition before *whom* can now sound stilted and over-formal:

? *I am left wondering at whom this book is aimed.*

A mixed style with *whom* and a preposition at the end is also unsatisfactory:

✗ *I am left wondering whom this book is aimed at.*

A common mistake is to prefer *whom* when *who* is in fact correct. This occurs in more complex relative clauses in which *who* seems to have a dual role:

✗ *This is the person whom Nancy claimed had attacked her.*
✓ *This is the person who Nancy claimed had attacked her.*

In this sentence, *whom* is not the object of the verb *claimed* but the subject of the clause *had attacked her*. The words *Nancy claimed* form a sort of aside, as can be seen if we separate it with punctuation:

✓ *This is the person who – Nancy claimed – had attacked her.*

Note also constructions in which a whole clause introduced by *who* is the object of a verb or preposition (in this case, *about*):

✗ *The team had a fierce argument about whom was responsible for the errors.*
✓ *The team had a fierce argument about who was responsible for the errors.*

What is the preposition *about* governing in this sentence? It appears to be the pronoun *who*, in which case we might expect *whom* to be correct, but look harder: what *about* is governing is the whole clause *who was responsible for the errors*, and within this clause the pronoun *who* is the subject of the verb *was*, and so not – by itself – the object of the preposition *about*.

Can whose *refer to a thing?*

*There were a few houses **whose** wrought-iron balconies were crammed with flowers.*

Some people object to using *whose* in this way to mean 'of which' instead of 'of whom', i.e. to refer to an inanimate thing rather than a person. But it is well established in ordinary usage and it is futile – and misconceived – to object to it.

See section 2, pp. 117–20, for **Wh-** words: **types of relative clause:** *that* or *which*?

Wh- words: interrogative pronouns and determiners

	things	function	person or people	function
singular and plural	*which* or *what*	pronoun and determiner	*who* or *whom*	pronoun
singular and plural			*what* or *which*	determiner
possessive	*whose*	pronoun and determiner	*whose*	pronoun and determiner

These words ask a question that seeks to identify a person or thing. Most of them can be used as pronouns (standing alone) or as determiners (with a noun), but *who* and *whom* are pronouns only and *what* and *which*, when used of a person, are determiners only (*what or which man?*):

pronoun	**What** did they say?
determiner	**What** new ideas do they have?
pronoun	**Who** was that?
pronoun	**Whom** did you see?
determiner	**Whose** car is that outside?
pronoun	**Whose** is that car outside?

They are also used in so-called **indirect questions**, in which the question is stated or implied rather as in indirect speech:

pronoun	Did you hear **what** they said?
determiner	Do we know **what** new ideas they have?
pronoun	I wonder **who** that was.
pronoun	I was curious about **whom** you saw.

determiner	*I don't know **whose** car that is outside.*
pronoun	*We must find out **whose** that car is outside.*

What or which?

The choice between *what* and *which* is straightforward when they are pronouns. *What* implies an open choice while *which* is used of a choice between a known or restricted number of options:

*We hardly knew **what** to do next.*
*He needed to know **which** he should bring.*

When they are determiners, however, standing before a noun (whether singular or plural), *what* and *which* are more interchangeable, but *which* is still more specific in tone than *what*:

***What** topics should we spend more time on?* (This suggests that the speaker is unsure about the range and limits of the choice.)
*Chris did not know **which** story she should read him.* (This suggests that the range of choice was known.)
***What** time did he say he'd meet you?* (The range of options is completely open, and *which* time would be unidiomatic here.)

Who's or whose?

Who's is a contracted form of *who is* or *who has*, used in conversational and less formal written English. It is used for both roles of *who*, as a relative pronoun and as an interrogative pronoun (in questions):

(relative) *It's not clear who's* [= who is] *to blame.*
(relative) *We don't know who's* [= who has] *been saying these things*.

(interrogative) *Who's* [= who is] *that over there?*
(interrogative) *Who's* [= who has] *done this?*

Take care to avoid confusing this use with the pronoun and determiner *whose*, which is used to show possession and is also both relative and interrogative:

(relative) *There were people whose families had died in the bombing.*
(interrogative) *Whose money is it anyway?*

Any, each, *and other indefinite words: determiners and pronouns*

determiners	pronouns	singular or plural?
any	*any*	both
each	*each*	mostly singular
every		singular
either	*either*	singular
neither	*neither*	both
	none	both
	anything, something, everything	singular
	anyone, anybody, someone, somebody, everyone, everybody	singular

The words listed above are various kinds of indefinite determiners and pronouns. *Any* can go with singular and plural nouns (*any bread, any places*), and is itself either singular or plural when standing alone as a pronoun. *None* functions only as a pronoun, as do those words ending in *-thing*, *-one*, and *-body*; *every* functions only as a determiner:

Every party has members in the Federal National Assembly.

Strictly speaking, *each*, *either*, and *neither* are singular words:

Each has her own lunchbox.
Either approach is valid.
Neither suggestion is the right one.

But when used on their own as pronouns, they can vary between singular and plural depending on whether the emphasis is on the individuals or on the collection or group as a whole, and *each* also has a special use following a plural noun or pronoun and becoming plural itself (as in the third example below):

(singular) *Either is preferable to having neither.*
(singular) *Neither the chairman nor the chief executive is planning any dramatic gestures.*
(plural) *They each last for several years.*
(plural) *Have either of you two ladies received an anonymous letter?*
(plural) *Neither of his parents earn much money any more.*

See **Pronouns**, p. 66, for *he or she* and alternatives.

Is none *singular or plural*?

The pronoun *none* causes particular doubts in users. There are people who insist that it is a singular pronoun and must therefore always be followed by a singular verb:

*None of the staff **was** able to identify the man later.*

But a plural verb is also possible:

*None of the staff **were** able to identify the man later.*

The purist view is wrongly based on the belief that *none* is a contraction of *no one*, whereas it is a later form of an Old English pronoun. In modern use it can stand for *no one* or *not any*. Whether it is followed by a singular or a plural verb depends on the sense. When the emphasis is on a single person or thing, you use a singular form of the verb:

*Ask your local authority if official approval is needed. If **none is** required, they will tell you.*
*Though the entrance hall is spacious, **none** of the rooms is large.*
*None of us **knows** absolutely why we know anything.*

When the main idea is of several people or things considered together, or an indefinite number, you should use a plural form of verb:

*We deal promptly with any complaints, but on this occasion there **were none**.*
*None of the council's social workers **have** attended the course.*
*She supposed they had no children, since **none were** mentioned.*

It is sometimes helpful to think of *none* in terms of *no*, which behaves in similar ways and can also go with singular or plural forms (*no money, no hope, no shoes, no crowds*).

A good apricot is eatable, which none from my garden are.

Jane Austen, *Mansfield Park*, 1814

And yet, of all poetry I know, none is so sorrowful as Scott's.

John Ruskin, *Modern Painters*, 1856

Each was miserably anxious . . . for some sign of the feeling that bound them together. But none was given.

Anthony Trollope, *Barchester Towers*, 1857

Myself *and* yourself: *reflexive pronouns*

person	singular	plural
first person	*myself*	*ourselves*
second person	*yourself*	*yourselves*
third person	*himself, herself, itself, oneself*	*themselves*

Note that the third person singular masculine form is *himself* and not (as you sometimes find) *his self*.

Reflexive pronouns formed with *-self* are used in sentences in which the subject of the verb and the object are the same person or thing, as in *We enjoyed ourselves* and *Make yourself at home*.

Themselves *(or* themself?*)*

A problem occurs when a reflexive pronoun refers back to a singular noun or pronoun of unknown or irrelevant gender. This problem is similar to the one we met when dealing with the possessive words *his, her,* and *their*:

✓ *They are considered to be too young to look after themselves.*

The use of the plural form *themselves*, as here, is a generally acceptable solution for ordinary speaking and writing. Waiting in the wings is a singular form *themself*, but this is at present non-standard:

✗ *They are considered to be too young to look after themself.*

In more precise writing, and in cases where it is important to preserve the individuality of the person referred to, the more traditional (but often unwieldy) alternative is:

✓ *The professional person is challenged to serve well and make a name for himself or herself.*

This approach is, however, difficult to maintain in a more prolonged sentence with further repetitions of the reference, and the result is often inconsistency:

? *Each human being strives to keep himself or herself going in their own particular character.*

By the time the writer of this sentence had to face a second reference back to the subject of the sentence ('each human being') he or she gave up, either consciously or unwittingly, and resorted to the indefinite plural form *their*. In a case like this it is better to recast the whole sentence in the plural:

✓ *All human beings strive to keep themselves going in their own particular character.*

In this version, everything falls naturally into place, and the sense is only slightly affected by the change.

Each other *and* one another: *reciprocal pronouns*

each other   one another

These pronouns can only be the objects (direct or indirect) of verbs, or follow prepositions such as *to* and *with*:

direct object	*The two men had known **each other** since their school days.*
after *with*	*Partners living together need to be open with **each other**.*
indirect object	*Sometimes we talk to the operators on submarines, and we send **each other** messages.*
after *to*	*The cabin crew clung to **each other** for support.*
after *into*	*The bedrooms all led into **one another**.*
direct *object*	*We must love **one another**, because if we don't we are likely to end up killing **one another**.*

You should not use *each other* or *one another* as the subjects of verbs:

✗ *In those days everyone knew who each other was.*
✓ *In those days everyone knew who everyone else was.*

Otherwise, *each other* and *one another* are largely interchangeable, despite the superstition (it is no more than that) that *each other* refers to two people or things and *one another* to more than two. This view receives no support in usage, and you can find plenty of examples in good writers that contradict it (see below). In the first two examples above the reference is to two people, whereas in the third and fourth examples there are more than two, or the number is indeterminate.

> *Every body differed, and every body was astonished at each other's opinion.*
>
> Jane Austen, *Sense and Sensibility*, 1811

> *I have endeavoured in this ghostly little book, to raise the ghost of an idea, which shall not put my readers out of humour with themselves, with each other, with the season, or with me.*
>
> Charles Dickens, *A Christmas Carol*, 1843

Although *each other* does not have to refer specifically to two, *one another* tends to imply more than two. If we say, for example, *Partners living together need to be open with one another*, we are probably thinking of more than one set of partners, although individually the relation is still between two people.

But this is by no means a hard-and-fast rule, as the following examples show:

*Occurring as matched pairs, they are mirror images of **one another**.*

*He heard the two men take their leave of **one another**.*

*Ever since they had known **one another**, Otto had been kind to Jean-Claude.*

We women do not love to hear one another's praises.

Henry Fielding, *Amelia*, 1752

In such a history events follow each other without necessarily having a connection with one another.

William Thackeray, *The Newcomes*, 1854

Knowing about prepositions

Prepositions are short words that show the relation between other words in a sentence. Typical examples are *about, by, in, near, on, under*, and *with*. Some pre-positions consist of more than one word, e.g. *close to, on top of*. They are normally followed by a noun or pronoun, or by a phrase:

*the shop **near** the station*
*a book **about** bees*
*candles **on top of** the cake*

Prepositions indicate several types of relation shown by the examples in the table (which is not a complete list):

place	*against, among, at, behind, below, beneath, beside, between, beyond, by, close to, down, from, in, inside, into, near, next to, off, on, on top of, opposite, out of, over, past, round, through, to, towards, upon, via, within*
time	*after, around, at, before, between, by, during, in, past, since, within*

relationship   *at, for, like, minus, on, per, plus, than, till, to, until, upon, with, without*

Ending a sentence with a preposition

Prepositions are normally followed by the noun or pronoun they relate to, or 'govern':

*She is **in** the garden.*
*Don't talk **to** him.*

But in some structures a preposition can become separated from its object, notably in questions and relative clauses:

*Which house do you live **in**?*
*This is the school I went **to**.*
*I need some paper to write **on**.*
*What did she think she was **up to**?*
*We weren't sure if the meal had been paid **for**.*

In these sentences, the prepositions *in, to, on, up to,* and *for* come at the end. This is the natural word order in English, and it differs in this respect from some inflected languages, including Latin, in which the preposition must always come before the word it governs. For this reason, grammarians in the 19th century decided that in English, as in Latin, prepositions should not be separated from their nouns and pronouns. They insisted on writing the sentences given above as follows:

In which house do you live?
This is the school to which I went.
I need some paper on which to write.

? *Up to what did she think she was?*

The last example is of course a nonsense that shows up the fallacy of trying to impose a Latinate rule on English. And the last sentence in the first group can't be turned round at all because the structure won't allow it. The other sentences are acceptable alternatives in the forms given in the second group, but so are the first versions given. You should not be afraid of forming sentences with prepositions at the end, even in writing, unless you want to sound consciously more formal.

This is the sort of English up with which I will not put.

Comment on avoiding prepositions at the end of sentences, attributed to Winston Churchill in the 1950s

Some words can be adverbs as well as prepositions. For example *down* is a preposition in the phrase *down the road*, and is an adverb in the phrase *look down*, and *in* is a preposition in the phrase *in the kitchen* and an adverb in the phrase *come in*. Other words of this type are:

above, across, after, along, around, before, behind, below, beneath, beside(s), between, beyond, by, inside, near, off, on, opposite, outside, over, past, round, since, through, throughout, to, under, underneath, up, within, without.

Other adverbs need support to become prepositions, e.g. *out* needs the support of the preposition *of* to make a new preposition *out of*, *next* needs the support of *to* to make *next to*, and *together* needs the support of *with* to make *together with*.

Out and out of

There is a special problem with *out*, because the rule differs on the two sides of the Atlantic. In British English, *out* is an adverb and the corresponding preposition is *out of*:

Do not lean out.
Do not lean out of the window.

In American English, *out* is also valid as a preposition, and you can say, for example:

Do not lean out the window.

But this is not acceptable in British English, except as a conscious Americanism.

On to or onto?
French windows opened onto the terrace.

Unlike *into*, which goes back to Old English, there is an aura of suspicion about combining *on* and *to* into a single preposition *onto*, even though it has been in use in this form since the early 17th century. If you are writing for someone who might be a language purist, it is best to avoid it, and write *on to*, which is never wrong.

There are also circumstances in which *onto* is definitely wrong:

• when the two words need to retain their own individual sense and do not have a combined meaning: *we moved on to the main road* means we went in that direction, whereas *we moved onto the main road* means we made contact with it.

• when *on* is closely linked to the verb it follows: *It was a while before we **cottoned on** to what she meant* (where *cottoned on* is a unit, called a **phrasal verb**).

The same rule applies, incidentally, to *into*, where *in to* is sometimes necessary:

They came in to loud applause.

Without *as a conjunction*

Without is a preposition and not a conjunction, so you cannot use it to introduce a clause:

✗ *Don't say anything without you mean it.*

The correct way of putting this is:

✓ *Don't say anything without meaning it.*

or:

✓ *Don't say anything unless you mean it.*

Without in the first of these alternatives is a preposition governing the verbal noun *meaning*, and is used correctly. In the second alternative, *unless*, which is a conjunction and can introduce a clause, is also used correctly. (You could also say . . . *if you do not mean it.*)

For more on conjunctions, see **Knowing about conjunctions** below.

Knowing about conjunctions

Conjunctions are joining words, used to link words and phrases rather like the cement in brickwork. The most familiar conjunctions are *and* and *but*, but there are others. (Notice that I have used both these conjunctions for real immediately after mentioning them in the previous sentence.) The third one that will be immediately familiar is *or*.

• Conjunctions can be used to link words:

*a friendly **and** devoted couple*
*poor **but** honest*
*choose one **or** other*

• They can also be used to link phrases and clauses:

*I opened the gate **and** went through.*
*She spoke slowly **but** they could still not understand her.*
*We could travel by car **or** take the train.*

In these sentences, conjunctions are used to link words and groups of words on an equal or balanced basis, in which the words before and after the conjunction have an equal status. This type is called a **coordinating conjunction**.
• There is another kind of conjunction, called a **subordinating conjunction**, which links a main clause to a subordinate clause. Typical subordinating conjunctions are *although, because, before, for, if, since, that, till, unless, until, when, where, whether, while,* and *why*:

*She was in control now, **because** she knew the truth.*
*You'd better read a chapter **before** we go out this afternoon.*

*It's vital **that** we contact them.*
*The father could be prosecuted **unless** the mother has sole custody.*
*I intend to find out **whether** she was there that night.*

• There are some conjunctions that are used in British English but not in American English:

*He decided to try to capture London **whilst** his troops were encamped on Kew Green.*
***Now** he was no longer alone he felt safer.*
*You cannot always be on hand **and nor** would you wish to be.*
*She was not frigid **but nor** had she ever been a slave to carnal temptations.*

And/or

And/or is a formula indicating that the items connected by it can be taken either together or as alternatives. Its principal uses are in legal and other formal documents, but in general use it is often clumsy:

The Press has rather plumped for the scholar as writer, and/or as bibliophile.

A more comfortable way of expressing the same idea is to use 'X or Y or both', and in some cases 'or' by itself will do.

But

But is both a preposition and a conjunction:

(preposition, = 'except') *You take orders from no one else **but** me.*
(conjunction, = 'except that') *You take orders from no one else **but** you take orders from me.*

(preposition, = 'except') *They have brought us nothing **but** misery*.

(conjunction, = 'although') *They have brought us nothing **but** they have brought us misery*.

These two roles that *but* has can cause uncertainty when pronouns (which change their form) are involved:

Everyone but he knows the truth.

or:

Everyone but him knows the truth.

There is no hard-and-fast rule about this, but the following points are recommended:

• When the phrase introduced by *but* relates closely to the subject of the sentence, you should treat the pronoun as a subject form (i.e. *No one knows but I*), but when the phrase is more closely related to the object, you should treat it like an object (i.e. *I told no one but him*).

• When the link is not as clear-cut as this, the choice of pronoun is decided by the position of the *but*-phrase in the sentence: when the *but*-phrase is in the area of the subject, treat the pronoun as a subject form (i.e. *Everyone but she can see the answer*) and when the *but*-phrase is in the area of the object treat the pronoun as an object (i.e. *Everyone can see the answer but her*).

• There is another difficult choice when the verb is intransitive and there is no object: *Everyone knows but her* is somewhat more natural than *Everyone knows but she*.

*He certainly has an eye to Emily, but behaves with
great prudence towards her: Yet everybody but she sees
his regard for her.*

Samuel Richardson, *Sir Charles Grandison*, 1754

*I could not have come through Canterbury to-day
without stopping, if I had been coming to anyone but
her.*

Charles Dickens, *David Copperfield*, 1850

either . . . or . . . *and* neither . . . nor . . .
In these uses, *either* and *or* and *neither* and *nor* are
paired conjunctions. Careful use is important, as there
are traps for the unwary.

• *Neither* should be followed by *nor*, not *or*:

There was neither food nor fuel in the house.
He is neither comic nor romantic enough for the role.
*The universe has no boundary. It is neither created nor
destroyed.*

• When the two alternatives are both plural, there is
no problem. They are collectively treated as plural:

Most of the mothers were either widows or deserted wives.
*Neither parents nor politicians are crying out for radical reform
of the system.*

• Nor is there a problem with many verbs that are the
same in the singular and plural:

*Either the government or the communities should take sole
responsibility.*

• If two singular alternatives are involved, you have a choice between treating them as singular or plural when the verb forms differ. This depends on whether the emphasis is on the two alternatives taken together or on each of them regarded separately:

(singular) *There is neither time nor machinery to do the job.*
(singular) *Neither the American nor most of the European press was subject to such restraints.*
(plural) *Neither the innkeeper nor the postmistress are paid in kisses.*

• A more awkward problem arises when one of the alternatives in an *either or . . .* or *neither . . . nor . . .* construction is singular and the other plural. In these cases, it is better to make the verb agree with the one closer to it:

✓ *Either the public authorities or the private market has had to make the necessary provision.*

But often an even better solution is to recast the sentence to avoid the problem:

✓ *Either the public authorities have had to make the necessary provision or the private market has.*

A mixture of persons normally has to be resolved by this kind of rephrasing:

? *Neither you nor your employer is likely to be a medical expert.*

is better as:

✓ *You are unlikely to be a medical expert and neither is your employer. (or . . . and nor is your employer.)*

Balancing the two halves of an either . . . or. . . *and* neither . . . nor . . . *sentence*

✓ *Either she's lying or she's crazy*
✓ *She is either lying or crazy*
✗ *She is either lying or she's crazy*

The last sentence is poorly formed because the two sides of the *either . . . or . . .* structure don't match. You can test this in your own writing by comparing what follows *either* with what follows *or*. In our last sentence, *either* is followed by the word *lying*, whereas *or* is followed by a complete clause *she's crazy*. In the first, *either* and *or* are both followed by balancing statements (*she's lying* and *she's crazy*), and in the second the balance is achieved by the corresponding words *lying* (which is a verbal adjective) and *crazy* (which is a simple adjective).

For

As a conjunction *for* can be used instead of *because* and *since*. It is generally more formal in effect, but it has two important limitations not shared by *because* or *since*:

• it cannot come at the beginning of a sentence but must follow a main clause:

I must have fallen asleep, for I dreamt that a girl was kissing me.

• it normally follows a comma, except occasionally when the sentence is short and the sense is more continuous:

Our activities did not go unnoticed, for we caught the eye of Mr Maple.

The matter did not end there for there were decisions to be made.

Beginning sentences with *and* or *but*

You do not often need to begin a sentence with a conjunction such as *and* or *but*. But the belief that it is always wrong is a superstition with no sound basis in grammar. (Note the beginning of my last sentence!) The practice is common in literature and can be effective:

Hortensio: *Are you a suitor to the maid you talk of – yea or no?*
Tranio: *And if I be, sir, is it any offence?*

William Shakespeare, *The Taming of the Shrew*, act I, scene ii

It is also used for other rhetorical purposes, especially to denote surprise (*And did you let him?*), to emphasize the force of what follows (as in my sentence above), or just to introduce an improvised afterthought (*I'm going to change my clothes. And don't you look*).

You will find several examples of *and* or *but* beginning sentences in this book.

When *and* where

When and *where* have a special role as conjunctions used to introduce an extra clause:

She had just finished her meal when the phone rang.
They went to London, where they met their uncle.

A comma is more usual before *where* than before *when*.

Determiners and quantifiers

These terms refer to a whole lot of very basic functional words that help to clarify or identify nouns. We have already met some words that are classed as **determiners**: for example, we saw that some demonstrative pronouns (*this*, *these*, etc.) could also stand as determiners before nouns, and so can *any*, *each*, and *every* (which has to). The words *a* and *an* (the indefinite article) and *the* (the definite article) are also determiners.

The following are the main determiners (note that 'singular' and 'plural' in the table refer to the nouns the words qualify, e.g. you can say *my book* and *my books*):

type	singular	plural
indefinite article	*a, an*	
definite article	*the*	*the*
demonstrative	*this, that*	*these, those*
possessive	*my, your, his, her, its, our, your, their*	*my, your, his, her, its, our, your, their*

The definite article: the

• Its principal use is to identify a person or thing already known or named:

*He put his bag on **the** table.*
*This is **the** one I mean.*

• It also has special uses, e.g. with proper nouns:

*His name was Charles Dickens. But he was not **the** Charles Dickens.*

The indefinite article: a, an

The role here is to identify a person or thing, usually one of many possible, that is not already known and has not already been named:

*He went to stay with **a** friend.*
*She had **a** pain.*
*Is that **a** spider?*

Quantifiers

There is another group of determiners that is sometimes called **quantifiers** because they refer to amount or extent:

singular	plural
all	*all*
any	*any*
	some
	both
each	
either	
enough	*enough*
every	
less	*less* or *fewer*, *least* or *fewest*
(a) little	
more	*more, most*
much	*many*
neither	
no	*no*
other	*other*
	several

Some quantifiers go with plural nouns (e.g. *both*, *few*, *many*, *several*), others go with singular nouns (e.g. *little*, *much*), and others again can go with either singular or plural nouns (e.g. *any*, *all*, *enough*, *more*, *most*, *no*). Some phrases, such as *a lot of* and *a number of*, are also sometimes classed as quantifiers.

For advice on *less* and *fewer*, see p. 268.

2
Building sentences

A number of sentences if emitted without interruption becomes a conversation. A conversation prolonged over an hour or more becomes a gossip. A gossip, when shared by several persons, is known as a secret.

Christopher Morley, *Mince Pie*, 1919

A sentence uttered makes a world appear Where all things happen as it says they do.

W H Auden, *Words*, 1956

A sentence is traditionally defined as a group of words that makes complete sense, contains a main verb (or one implied), and in print or writing begins with a capital letter and ends with a full stop, question mark, or exclamation mark as appropriate. We can argue the toss over the details, but the key feature of a sentence is that it is independent in terms of grammar, and 'not linked by virtue of any grammatical construction to any larger linguistic form'. (The words are those of the distinguished American linguist Leonard Bloomfield, written in 1933. They sum it up perfectly.)

Language is made up of a sequence of sentences. This is true of both spoken and written language, although the structure is much more obvious when it is written. The sentence is the main unit of expression in most languages, and is made up of a number of words and groups of words (phrases). A sentence can make a statement, ask a question, give an instruction, or simply make an exclamation. A group of sentences makes up a paragraph, which normally deals with a single main idea. The paragraph you are now reading contains six sentences (including this one) and its main idea has been to tell you what a sentence *does* (whereas the previous paragraph defined what a sentence *is*) and why it is important.

What you want to say: types of sentences

The way you organize your sentence depends in the first place on the type of thing you want to say: on whether, for example, you are stating something or asking a question. Here are some examples of different types of sentences:

statement	*Tanya runs an agency.*
question	*Have you eaten?*
instruction	*Try and relax.*
exclamation	(also called an **interjection**) *God forbid!*

You will see that the punctuation provides information about the type of sentence in each case. Statements end in full stops, questions in question marks, and exclamations in exclamation marks. Like all punctuation, these marks are there to help the reader understand the meaning that the writer intends to convey.

A typical statement contains a verb (a word denoting an action, e.g. *open*, *eat*, or a state, e.g. *be*, *seem*), a subject, which is the person or thing that performs the action (e.g. *Tanya* in the statement above or *you* in the question), and often an object, which is the person or thing affected by the action (e.g. *an agency* in the first sentence).

A plan of the first sentence would look like this:

subject	verb	object
Tanya	*runs*	*an agency.*

Because *run* has an object, *an agency*, it is called a **transitive** verb. Other verbs can express actions without having any object, e.g. many of the words expressing movement, such as *come*, *go*, *walk*, etc. And some verbs can be both transitive and intransitive; for example, *run*, which we saw taking an object in the last example, can be used without one in other meanings:

subject	verb	object
Tanya	*was running.*	

(For more on transitive and intransitive verbs, see **Knowing about verbs** in section 1, p. 17).

The parts of a sentence classed as verb and object (if any) are also collectively called the **predicate**.

Some verbs don't express an action but a state:

The days are long and dark.

In this sentence, *long and dark* is called the **complement** of the verb *are*, because it completes the sense. Without it the sentence would make no sense at all:

The days are.

The complement *long and dark* therefore completes the sense:

subject	verb	complement
The days	*are*	*long and dark.*

It is also possible to have sentences without verbs, because the verb is 'understood' from something previously said: '*Will you meet me tomorrow?*' '*OK.*' (= OK, I will meet you tomorrow) (This practice is very common and will be familiar: it is called **ellipsis** and is discussed in more detail on p. 130.)

The long and short of it: different sentence structures

The types of sentence that we have just been looking at have to do with the kind of thing being said, e.g. whether it is a statement or a question. There is another classification which has more to do with the structure of each sentence, i.e. the way it is put together with nouns, verbs, conjunctions, and so on:

• a **simple** sentence, normally containing a single statement: *Moira put down the phone.*

• a **compound** sentence containing more than one statement, normally joined by a conjunction such as *and* or *but*:

Moira put down the phone and went over to the window.
I used to live in London but last year I moved to Glasgow.

• a **complex** sentence containing a main clause and one or more clauses that depend on it (called **subordinate**), such as a conditional clause beginning with *if* or a relative clause introduced by *which* or *who* or *that*:

Your solicitor will do a local search if you buy a property.
This is a matter that needs to be considered afresh.
When Janet was 14 months old her brother Francis was born.

In compound sentences, each part can stand by itself and makes sense if detached from the rest of the sentence, e.g. *Moira went over to the window, I moved to Glasgow.* Compound sentences can also be formed with a semicolon or colon, which makes the separate grammatical identity of each part even clearer:

She became devoted to Francis; she loved the way his beret sat on his round head.
The children often visited Beatrice: she was a friendly black pig.

With longer sentences containing a lot of commas, a semicolon is useful for making a compound sentence when you don't want to make two sentences:

Her hair grew wilder and frizzier, escaping from its pigtails, tangling in everything it touched; her hair ribbons fell off, her buttons pinged to the floor, she tripped over and collided with objects so often that she had to have a special eyesight test.

In complex sentences, on the other hand, the subordinate clauses make no sense by themselves:

? *if you buy a property*
? *that needs to be considered afresh*

There are often several ways of expressing the same basic idea or fact, using either compound or complex sentences. Compound sentences tend to make each statement of equal value, whereas complex sentences, which involve one clause subordinated to another, put a slant on what you are saying:

(compound) *Moira put down the phone and went over to the window.*
(complex) *When Moira had put down the phone she went over to the window.*
(compound) *I used to live in London but in 2000 I moved to Glasgow.*
(complex) *Although I used to live in London I have lived in Glasgow since 2000.*

These – and other – different ways of building sentences affect the balance and emphasis of your writing. And unlike speech, which is more or less instant, when you put ideas into writing you have time to pause and organize your material and to try different ways until you find the one that is most suitable for what you want to say. How you connect facts and ideas is one key to clear and effective writing.

The comma splice

You should not normally use a comma to tack on a second distinct statement that is complete in itself:

I saw someone lying on the pavement, they weren't moving.

This practice, called the comma splice, is very common but is not good style – except sometimes for special effect in dramatic narrative – and is widely regarded as incorrect. The correct way of organizing this sentence is with a conjunction such as *and*:

I saw someone lying on the pavement, and they weren't moving.

or with a semicolon or colon:

I saw someone lying on the pavement right outside the court: they weren't moving.

or in a simpler and neater form with slight rephrasing:

I saw someone lying on the pavement and not moving.

or with a relative pronoun (in this case, *who*):

I saw someone lying on the pavement who wasn't moving.

(The last two ways of doing it have the advantage of eliminating the problem of needing a gender-neutral pronoun that can refer back to *someone*, a problem we looked at in the previous section under the heading **Knowing about pronouns**, p. 66.)

How it all fits: word order

In English, the order of the words in a sentence is vital to understanding its meaning, because unlike some other languages the forms of the words themselves do not always change to show their function in the sentence: for example, whether a noun like *dog* or *man* is the subject or object of the verb: there is a vast difference between *the dog bit the man* (in which *dog* is the subject, i.e. performed the action, and *man* is the object, i.e. was the recipient of the action) and *the man bit the dog* (in which *man* is the subject and *dog* is the object).

The normal word order of an English sentence is subject–verb–object:

subject	verb	object
She	*saw*	*her chance.*

An adverb or adverb phrase, or more than one, might come at the end:

subject	verb	object	adverb phrase
She	*saw*	*her chance*	*at last.*

subject	verb	adverb phrase 1	adverb phrase 2
The girls	*went*	*to the village*	*that morning.*

Each of these elements can consist of a single word or a group of words. In the last example, there is no object, because the verb is **intransitive**, i.e. its meaning doesn't involve an action affecting someone or something else: most verbs of movement and state have these kinds of meaning.

The order of words is sometimes changed by a process called 'inversion' in sentences such as *There goes the last bus* and in quoted speech such as *'Over here!' called the man*.

There are more complex rules of word order that we normally observe instinctively: for example, an adverbial expression of place normally comes before an adverbial expression of time, as in the village example above.

Changing the order: inversion
Inversion occurs when the normal order of words in a statement is reversed so that a less usual word comes first.

Normal sentence order is often reversed in questions:

Did you remember to bring a towel?
Was the exercise difficult?

But the order remains unchanged when the question begins with an interrogative word such as *who* and *what*:

Who wrote this?

Word order can also be varied in statements. The point of this is to emphasize the word that is moved to the beginning:

Easy this isn't.
Home she went in mutinous silence.

Some forms of inversion are less dramatic than this. Compare this simple statement:

I go to the swimming pool on Wednesdays.

with the same statement in this form:

On Wednesdays I go to the swimming pool.

In the first version, the fact of going swimming is the main point of the statement. In the second version, the time factor, by being placed at the beginning as the first thing the listener hears or the reader sees, has become the main point of the statement. If we were to put a comma after Wednesdays, separating the adverbial phrase more emphatically, the effect would be even greater:

On Wednesdays, I go to the swimming pool.

There are other routine forms of inversion in English:

• in direct speech, the quoted words can be followed by a statement of who spoke them, using a 'reporting' verb such as *say, ask, remark, reply, shout,* etc., either in normal order or in inverted order:

'Are you there?' he asked.
'I'm over here,' replied Anne.

Inversion is normally only possible when a noun (e.g. *Anne, the woman*) goes with the reporting verb, and not when there is a pronoun instead of a noun (e.g. *he* in the first sentence above). Expressions such as *asked he* and *said she* – which were once more common – now sound dated and affected unless they are deliberately imitating older usage.

• in negative statements, the negative word can come first, with the rest of the sentence inverted:

Never had he seen such chaos.
Nor would they ever return.

• in conditional statements, *if* and *whether* can be omitted and this part of the condition can be expressed by inversion:

Had they known this, their answer would have been different.
They must be treated the same, be they adults or children.
(Note the use of the subjunctive *be* in the second case, which unlike the first is an 'open' condition in which the condition is capable of being fulfilled.)

• statements can be reinforced with the verb *do* in an inverted afterthought or aside:

He liked his beer, did Gerald.

• inversion can occur after an adjective intensified by the word *so*:

He could hardly remember his own name, so nervous was he.

Making it all fit together: agreement

When we use words together in sentences, we often have to change their form so that they fit together and produce the right grammar and meaning. In the sentence *John wants me to give you these flowers*, *wants* is the form of the verb *want* that agrees with its subject *John* and *give* is the form that goes with *to*. The word *these* is a plural form to agree with its noun *flowers*, and the pronoun *me* is in the first person because it refers to the speaker. This process of making words fit the context of sentences is called **agreement** or, more technically, **concord**.

For most of the time we apply the rules of agreement instinctively, just as we seem to find the right words in our mind when we need them. But problems can arise from time to time. Sometimes words have special meanings that do not seem to correspond to their grammatical form. When we mix words about with other words in sentences we can easily lose mental track and link the wrong words together, especially in conversation when we have less time to think and fewer opportunities to correct mistakes.

Awkward sentences

In some sentences, especially longer ones, the subject can be singular but separated from its verb by other words that happen to be in the plural. This can lead you to put the verb in the plural as well, and this is incorrect:

✗ *The consequence of long periods of inactivity or situations in which patients cannot look after themselves are often quite severe and long-lasting.*

Here, the string of plural nouns coming before the main verb *are* has caused the writer to lose sight of the real subject of the sentence, which is *consequence*. To make the sentence correct, we have three choices: to change *consequence* to *consequences*, to change *are* to *is*, or to recast the sentence more simply; for example:

✓ *Long periods of inactivity or situations in which patients cannot look after themselves can often have quite severe and long-lasting consequences.*

Here is another example from a recent newspaper article:

✗ *Like the Benin bronzes or the Ashanti regalia or the Stone of Scone, the location of such national icons matter deeply to those who once owned them.*

The subject of the verb *matter* (i.e. the thing that the word *matter* is about) is the singular noun *location*, and so *matter* should be *matters*:

✓ *The location of such national icons matters deeply to those who once owned them.*

You can see what happened here. The writer has been distracted by using the plural noun *icons* into thinking that a plural verb is needed, forgetting that the true subject is not *icons* but *location*, which is further back in the sentence.

Losing track

Another thing that often happens is that you can lose track halfway through a sentence and produce something that doesn't fit together properly:

✗ *Mr Howard's methods of tackling crime are outdated, illiberal, and will not work.*

In this sentence, we expect another describing word or phrase after *illiberal*, but we get a new verb *will* even though the earlier one, *are*, is still affecting (or 'governing', to use the technical term) this part of the sentence. A correct version of this sentence would read:

✓ *Mr Howard's methods of tackling crime are outdated and illiberal, and will not work.*

Awkward phrases

Some expressions can cause uncertainty because they are grammatically ambiguous or combine seemingly contradictory roles, e.g. phrases such as *more than one* and *either or both*:

More than one site is available.

The meaning is clearly plural, but the grammar remains singular because *one* is closer to the verb as well as being the dominant word in its phrase (we could not say *More than one site are available* although this is valid logically).

? *Tickets are valid for either or both performances.*

Here there is a problem of agreement with the following noun, because *either* calls for the singular form *performance* whereas *both* calls for the plural form *performances*; *both* wins out because it is closer to the noun. Usually a better solution is to adjust or recast the sentence to avoid the problem altogether:

✓ *Tickets are valid for either or both of the performances.*

There is a similar problem with *one or more*:

? *The bacteria can cause infection in one or more joints of the body.*

Again a small adjustment gets round the difficulty:

✓ *The bacteria can cause infection in one or more of the joints of the body.*

Kind of –, sort of –

This very common little expression is used to indicate a class or category of people or things, as in *a kind of cheese*, *this kind of house*, and *that sort of man*. Problems arise when it is followed by a plural noun, and language purists tend to insist on making the generic word *kind*, *sort*, or *type* plural as well, e.g. *these kinds of houses*, *those sorts of men*. But you will often find a mixed style, e.g. *these kind of houses*, *those sort of men* (with the plural forms *these* and *those* beside the singular form *kind* and *sort*), and you may well be tempted to use this style yourself, because it is so common.

This mixed style is acceptable in informal speech, because the plural word (*houses*, *men*) effectively take over as the subject, taking the role of 'head' of the phrase and attracting the verb to it and away from the generic word. The generic phrases *kind of* and *sort of* are then regarded as asides. So there is a logical justification for the mixed style, but it is best to avoid it in more formal writing and in official contexts, because it is often frowned on and you will not normally have the chance to defend it. And, to be frank, it can sound a little sloppy.

The recommended alternative is to use the plural forms *kinds of* and *sorts of*, or to rephrase slightly by putting *of this kind* or *of this sort* after the plural word:

houses of this sort, men of that kind. This option can be preferable, especially when the use of a plural *kinds* or *sorts* is obviously an artificial means of coping with the grammatical problem, and does not genuinely reflect a plural idea (as perhaps in the second sentence below).

Here are some further examples of doubtful (**?**) and recommended (✓) usage:

? *I think these kind of comments are most unfair.*
✓ *I think these kinds of comments are most unfair.*
✓ *I think comments of this kind are most unfair.*

? *The women's liberation movement builds on those kind of feelings.*
✓ *The women's liberation movement builds on those kinds of feelings.*
✓ *The women's liberation movement builds on feelings of that kind.*

? *Those sort of people eat far too much starch.*
✓ *Those sorts of people eat far too much starch.*
✓ *People of that sort eat far too much starch.*

Egg and chips: *compound subjects*

Two nouns joined by *and* are normally treated as plural:

Speed and accuracy are paramount.

But when the two nouns form a phrase that can be regarded as a single unit, they are sometimes (or, when the unity is very strong, always) treated as singular even when one of them is plural:

Egg and chips is my favourite meal.
This Antony and Cleopatra is the best I have seen.

In the second example, a plural is not possible because the title is equivalent to a singular word such as *play* or *performance*. What the writer is saying here is that this *performance of Antony and Cleopatra* is the best he has seen. This more generic word that can replace a more specific or complex one is often called the 'notional subject'.

This practice, which is very old in English, can extend to concepts that are distinct in themselves but are regarded as a single item in a particular sentence. However, it is best to regard this as a literary or rhetorical device and avoid it in everyday writing and speaking:

*The quality and skill of the frontline troops **is** what matters.*
*The extent and severity of drug use in the city **has been** a severe shock.*

When a singular noun forming the subject of a sentence is followed by an additional element tagged on by means of a phrase such as *as well as, accompanied by*, or *together with*, the following verb should be singular and not plural, since the singular noun is by itself the true subject:

*A diary of meetings, together with advance notices of forthcoming events, **appears** at the end of the report.*
*(But note A diary of meetings and advance notices of forthcoming events **appear** at the end of the report.)*
*Your application, accompanied by proof of identity, **needs** to be sent to the licensing authority.*

(But note *Your application and proof of identity **need** to be sent to the local licensing authority*.)

Wh- words: relative clauses

The *wh-* words we are concerned with here are *who* (or *whom*), *which,* and *whose.* We looked at their forms and main uses in section 1. Here we can see how they link parts of a sentence in different ways in relative clauses; for example:

She showed me the chair which was broken.

Two types of relative clause

There are two types of relative clause, called 'restrictive' and 'non-restrictive'. A **restrictive** (or **defining**) **clause** gives defining or identifying information about a noun or noun phrase that comes before, and is essential to the structure and sense of the sentence. In the sentence given above, 'the chair' is defined or identified as 'the one which (or that) was broken', and distinguished from other chairs that were not broken.

Compare the following sentence:

She showed me the chair, which was broken.

In this form, the information in the relative clause introduced by *which* is extra information that could be left out without affecting the structure or meaning of the sentence: the chair she showed me happened to be broken but this fact is not used to identify the chair concerned. This type of clause is called a **non-restrictive clause.**

The punctuation is important: restrictive or defining

clauses should not have a comma before them, while non-restrictive or non-defining clauses should have a comma to mark the pause you make in speech with such clauses and to make it clear that the clause is not defining the preceding noun. Here are some more examples of each type of clause:

restrictive	*The writer tries to explore some of the factors **which** influence our disposition to commit crimes.*
restrictive	*Thanks to all the readers **who** replied.*
non-restrictive	*The sides were organized by the army, **who** also provided playing facilities.*
non-restrictive	*The water passed from the mill into the little river Swilgate, **which** wends its way through the fields towards Tewkesbury.*
restrictive	*It is important to see customers **whose** patronage provides your regular income.*
non-restrictive	*He was utterly ignorant of the involvement of his family, **whose** name he had abandoned.*

In several of the non-restrictive examples, you can see how useful a relative clause can be in introducing information which continues the thread of the description or the narrative of the story.

A non-restrictive clause can also apply to a whole clause and not just the preceding noun or noun phrase:

The sun came out, which was welcome.

> ### Using an -ing verb instead
>
> An alternative to the restrictive type of relative clause is to use a participle, an -*ing* form of the verb:
>
> *The writer tries to explore some of the factors **influencing** our disposition to commit crimes.*
> *There were several people **wanting** to meet her.*
>
> This is often neater, especially in shorter sentences where a full-blown relative clause might be unwieldy.

That or *which*?

In restrictive clauses, you can often use the generic relative word *that* in place of *which*, *who*, or *whom*, and it is often the more natural choice in everyday writing and conversation, especially in place of *which*:

She showed me the chair that was broken instead of *She showed me the chair which was broken.*
The children that had been playing outside were now gone instead of *The children who had been playing outside were now gone.*

There are occasions when *that* is more idiomatic than *which*, e.g. when the construction is based on an impersonal *it* or an indefinite pronoun such as *anything*:

*There is something **that** I wanted to say.*
*Is there anything **that** you need?*

That is also more usual when *which* already occurs earlier in the sentence in another role, e.g. as an interrogative word:

*Which is the one **that** you like best?*

But you cannot use *that* in a non-restrictive clause following a comma:

✗ *She showed me the chair, that I saw was broken.*
✓ *She showed me the chair, which I saw was broken.*

Omission of that
When *that* is the object of a verb, it can be omitted:

*Is there anything **that** you need?* or (less formal) *Is there anything you need?*
*The moment **that** we had all dreaded arrived* or (less formal) *The moment we had all dreaded arrived.*

That offers one very useful advantage: it can replace both *who* (or *whom*) and *which*. This makes it invaluable in mixed sentences such as the following:

*These are the people and the ideas **that** most demand our attention.*

But *that* cannot be used after a preposition, such as *at* or *to*:

*This is the section **to which** the change applies* or (less formal) *This is the section the change applies to.*
*He was the person **with whom** she planned to spend the rest of her life* or (less formal) *He was the person she planned to spend the rest of her life with.*

Negatives and double negatives

Repeated negatives of the type *He never did no harm to no one* are regarded as illiterate in current English, and they should be avoided. They are not intrinsically wrong, and some languages use repeated negatives to strengthen the effect. Indeed, they were once a regular feature of standard English, and are to be found in Chaucer, Shakespeare, and other writers up to the 17th century. The logic then changed, and a sequence of negatives came to be regarded as self-cancelling instead of reinforcing each other.

But a double negative is acceptable when it is used as a kind of figure of speech with intentional cancelling effect, as in *It has not gone unnoticed* (= It most certainly has been noticed).

Double negatives are also acceptable, especially in speech, in uses of the type *You can't not go* (= You cannot consider not going, i.e. You have to go), in which *not go* is effectively a verb phrase expressing an integrated idea. But such strong feeling exists against repeated negatives that it is often more prudent to rephrase this type of sentence, especially in more formal or official writing. For example, you could say *You can't avoid going* (or simply *You have to go*).

Using the subjunctive

The **subjunctive** is normally associated with the classical languages, especially Latin, but it still exists in English (particularly American English), although its role is much more limited. It is a special form (or mood) of a verb expressing a wish or possibility instead of fact:

*Zeus granted the boy immortality on condition that he **remain** for ever slumbering.*
*James II decreed that Protestants **be persecuted** in their turn.*

In these sentences, the verbs *remain* (in the first) and *be persecuted* (in the second) are in the subjunctive; the ordinary forms (called the **indicative**) would be *remains* and *are persecuted*. The subjunctive form is recognizable in English only in the third person singular present tense, which omits the final -*s*, and in the forms *be* and *were* of the verb *be*.

In many cases, an alternative construction with *should* or *might* can also be used, and in some cases a simple form of the verb (e.g. *is* instead of *be*):

*It was important that he **should be included** [or **is included**] in my photographs.*
*James II decreed that Protestants **should be persecuted** in their turn.*

There are other typical uses of the subjunctive. In most cases alternative patterns not involving the subjunctive are also possible:

• after *if* (or *as if*, *as though*, or *unless*) in open conditions:

*Each was required to undertake that if it **were** chosen it would place work here.*
(Also possible: *if it was chosen . . .*)

• *be* or *were* placed at the beginning of a clause with the subject following it:

Were he to be challenged the choice of weapons would be his.
(Also possible: *If he was challenged . . .*)
*Professional agencies look to our problems, **be** they medical, psychological, or moral.*
(Also possible: *whether they are medical, psychological, or moral.*)

• in negative constructions, with *not* (or *never*, etc.) normally placed before the subjunctive verb, so that the subjunctive status of the verb is recognizable in the first and second persons as well as the third:

*He suggested that we not **make** any further comment.*
(Also possible: *. . . that we should not make any further comment.*)
*One essential quality for a holiday novel is that it not **be** too light.*
(Also possible: *. . . that it should not be too light.*)

• in certain fixed expressions and phrases, e.g. *as it were, be that as it may, come what may, far be it from me, God save the Queen, heaven forbid, perish the thought, so be it.*

The subjunctive is also used in some conditional clauses after *if* or *unless* (see the next section).

If-clauses

If is a conjunction that can introduce subordinate clauses (i.e. clauses dependent on a main clause). It has two main roles that look similar:

• *If* can introduce subordinate clauses that contain a condition: these are called **conditional clauses**. Conditional clauses can come first in the sentence, before the main clause, or they can come after the main clause:

If you do that you'll break it.
If she saw Harry there she'll tell us.
I'd be pleased *if you could come with me*.

There are two types of conditional clauses:

real conditions: those that can possibly be the case (or have been the case) in the present, past, or future (as in the sentences above). These can also refer to repeated or constant eventualities:

If you pay online you get an email acknowledgment.
We always saw Dan's family *if we went down to the beach*.
If you need help, you shall have it.

In real conditions referring to the future, you can use the verbs *should* or *were to* (the subjunctive: see below) or *was to*. This use suggests uncertainty or tentativeness, although the condition is still a possible one:

If he should (or *were to* or *was to*) *die first*, what will you do?

unreal conditions: those that could not be the case (or could not have been the case):

*What would you do **if I were** [or **was**] **not here** [but I am]?*
*If I **had the time** [but I don't] I'd give you a piece of my mind.*
*If I **were you** [but I'm not] I would have a pretty shrubbery.*

The last example illustrates the common idiom *if I were you*. *Were* is a survival of the English subjunctive, and is also used in the first example, although there you could use *was* instead. With unreal conditions in the present, you use the past tense in the *if*-clause and *would* or *should* or *might* in the main clause.

With unreal conditions in the past, you use the past perfect (or pluperfect, with *had*) in the *if*-clause and *would have, should have, could have*, or *might have* in the main clause:

*If **we had arrived earlier** we could have had a drink at the bar first.*
*I could have helped you **if only you'd said something**.*

• *If*-clauses also introduce so-called **indirect questions**, which are reported questions and also ways of asking questions indirectly:

*She asked **whether** [or **if**] you had seen anything of her sister.*
*I don't know **whether** [or **if**] I'll still be here then.*
*I wonder **whether** [or **if**] you'd help me with these bags?*

The same construction with *if* or *whether* is also used after verbs that express consideration and reflection (such as *consider, decide*, and *discuss*) or uncertainty (principally *doubt* and *wonder*). *Whether* is more usual with the considering verbs, and is obligatory when it is followed by a *to*-infinitive, as in the first example below. *If* and *whether* are largely interchangeable after the verbs expressing uncertainty:

*I'll decide **whether** [**✗ if**] to go in the morning.*
*Will you discuss **whether** [**? if**] you are free to come.*
*We wondered **whether** [or **if**] they might like to come too.*

May *and* might
Choice between *may* and *might* can cause confusion when used with conditional *if*-clauses:

*If things don't improve soon, you **may** need to find another employer.*
*It **may** help if you put the light on.*

In this kind of so-called 'open' conditional referring to the future, i.e. one which is capable of being fulfilled, *might* can be used in place of *may*. The sentences above could also be written as follows:

*If things don't improve soon, you **might** need to find another employer.*
*It **might** help [= would probably help] if you put the light on.*

Sometimes the *if*-clause is implied rather than stated, but the effect on *may* and *might* is the same:

*You **may** need to find another employer.*
*You **might** need to find another employer.*

There is little difference in meaning, although there is a greater element of supposition and remoteness with *might*.

When they refer to the past, *may* and *might* are used

with *have*, and there is a bigger difference between *may have* and *might have*.

May have is used when it is open whether the event or circumstance was in fact the case. When there is no *if*-clause, *may have* and *might have* are mostly interchangeable in the same way as *may* and *might* are when referring to the future, as we saw above:

*I **may have** dropped it in the corridor.*
*I **might have** dropped it in the corridor.*

But *might* usually reduces the likelihood that the event happened, and in some contexts eliminates it:

*You **may have** been hurt.* (and we should check)
*You **might have** been hurt.* (but you weren't)

When there is an *if*-clause, or one strongly implied, the choices are more clear-cut.

May implies a real possibility:

*If they were there, they **may have** seen what happened.* (= it is possible that they saw)

Might implies a possibility that was not in fact the case and is now therefore unreal:

*If you had told us we **might not have** wasted our time finding out.* (you didn't and we have)
With proper care [= if we had taken proper care] *we **might have** avoided this problem.* (but we didn't)

The main trap to avoid falling into is using *may have* instead of *might have* to denote an unreal possibility in the past:

✗ *Better advice **may have** prevented her from making a faux pas on her first day, when she wore a skirt that was much too short.*

Clearly she did not receive better advice, and she did commit the faux pas. So the word needed here is not *may* but *might*:

✓ *Better advice **might have** prevented her from making a faux pas on her first day . . .*

May have and *might have* are also used to refer to events possibly completed in the future, and here they are interchangeable:

*I **may have** finished this by tomorrow.*
*I **might have** finished this by tomorrow.*

Direct and indirect speech

There are two ways of giving the words of other people in writing. These are called direct speech and indirect speech. In **direct speech**, the actual words used are reproduced with quotation marks (also called inverted commas):

'Just look at that,' said Grimes.
'It's time Paul and I were going,' he said.
'He certainly didn't look ill,' said Harriet, 'in fact quite the contrary.'
'How many people live here?' she asked.
'Splendid!' said Paul. 'It's much the best thing you can do.'

The originator of the words is indicated by a so-called reporting verb such as *say, answer, reply, think*, etc.

Some reporting verbs carry special shades of meaning, e.g. to give emphasis (*state, declare, announce, remark, utter, assert, maintain*) or to indicate special kinds of speaking (*whisper, mumble, mutter*) or mood (*shout, bawl, grumble*). Note the punctuation when the reporting verb interrupts the quoted words, which is a common device in narrative writing: the quotation marks normally go outside the punctuation that belongs to the spoken words, as with the commas in the first three examples, the question mark in the fourth, and the exclamation mark in the fifth.

In **indirect** or **reported speech**, the words are taken over or 'reported' by the writer or speaker, and the tense (present, past, or future) and person (*I, you, she,* etc.) are made to conform to the reporting writer's or speaker's point of view rather than that of the originator of the words:

*He said that it **was** time he and Paul were going.*
*She asked how many people **lived** there.*

In the last sentence, you could say *She asked how many people live there*, which implies a greater sense of continuity and places less emphasis on the actual time the original words were used. Everything depends on the perspective of the reporting relative to the original use of the words.

Choice of tense (called 'sequence of tenses') becomes more complex in indirect or reported speech. Here, the tense of the reported action changes in accordance with the time perspective of the speaker:

*He said that it **was** time he and Paul **were going.***

However, the tense of the reported verb can stay the same if the time in which the speaker is operating is the same as that in which the reported person operates: *She **likes** making jam* can be converted either to *She said she **liked** making jam* or to *She said she **likes** making jam*, and *I **won't be coming** again* can be converted either to *I said I **wouldn't be coming** again* or to *I said I **won't be coming** again*.

In the sentence given above, it would be possible to say *She asked how many people **live** there*. In this case, the time perspective of the reported words is in the past, but the time perspective of their reference continues into the present, i.e. to the time of reporting.

Omission of that

In everyday speech, and even in writing, you can routinely leave out the conjunction *that* in reported speech. If you do this, the meaning is still clear:

*He said it **was** time he and Paul **were going***

Leaving words out
The verbless sentence
Most sentences contain a verb, but it is possible to have a sentence in which the verb is 'understood' without being expressed, by a process we call **ellipsis**, in which omitted words or even whole sentences are supplied from what has gone before.

'Are you still married?' 'Yes.' (= 'Yes, I am still married.')
This report from our Moscow correspondent. (= 'This report is from (*or* comes from) our Moscow correspondent' in a radio or television news bulletin.)

Some sentences consist of single-word or single-phrase exclamations:

'Sarah!'
'Goodness me!'

Ellipsis in narratives

The openings of some well-known novels contain verb-less sentences for special effect, e.g. the famous scene-setting beginning of Charles Dickens' *Bleak House*:

London. Michaelmas Term lately over, and the Lord Chancellor sitting in Lincoln's Inn Hall. Implacable November weather.

Narratives often rely on verbless sentences to avoid tedious repetition and make the action develop faster:

She wouldn't get rid of a perfectly good husband and a title to marry me. Not by divorce. Certainly not by conniving at murder.

Afterthoughts in narratives are often presented in this way too:

That way, they can work out their aggressions. Once a year.

Another device is to leave out the subject of the sentence, especially when this is the first person (*I*). This is especially common in the literary technique called 'interior monologue', in which the writer addresses readers with an informal narrative of thoughts rather in the manner of a personal diary:

Woke around five, my head still thick from booze and cigarettes. Bit of a carry-on last night! Thought of her face at the pub doorway.

This resembles the practice of everyday speech:

Glad you liked it.
Sorry to have to tell you this.

This is good natural English in the right place, i.e. in creative writing, but is too casual in tone for more formal contexts such as business letters or job applications.

Other types of omission

When you have a sentence made up of a string of verbs all having the same subject, it is usual to omit the subject on repeated occurrences:

Anna didn't answer her, but ∧ rose from the floor, ∧ lifted the bucket and ∧ threw the soapy water into the sink.

The verb itself is often omitted after *to* or after an auxiliary verb when another occurs immediately after it:

She did not say a word, although she would dearly have liked to ∧.
Peaceful cooperation between them can ∧ and must develop.

The relative pronoun *that* or *which* is routinely omitted

informally, especially when a final preposition (in this case, *in*) refers back:

This place reminds me of the holiday house ∧ I used to stay in.

The verb *be* is often omitted, especially in informal English, when it can be understood from an earlier occurrence in the same role:

They are relieved to know that and ∧ anxious to help.
She was expecting a visit and ∧ looking forward to it.

But when *be* is used in different roles in the same sentence, for example as an auxiliary verb and then as a linking verb followed by an adjective, it must be repeated because its role is different:

*He **was** making the dinner and **was** happy to do it.*

This is all fine – and idiomatic – when your hearer or reader can reasonably be expected to supply the missing words from the rest of the sentence without causing confusion. In ordinary conversation most uses of ellipsis go unnoticed because it is such a common feature of English. But ellipsis is less satisfactory, and in some cases not possible, when the omitted word does not have the same form and function as it does where it is present in the sentence:

? *We will try to arrange things better than they have been ∧ up to now.* (The word to be supplied is *arranged*, not *arrange*.)
✓ *We will try to arrange things better than they have been **arranged** [or done] up to now.*

✗ *We doubt whether a person such as Miss Havisham ever has ∧ or will exist.* (The word to be supplied after *has* is *existed*, not *exist*.)

✓ *We doubt whether a person such as Miss Havisham ever has **existed** or will exist.*

✗ *What I want from my life is every bit as important ∧, if not more so, than what John wants.*

(The words *as important* should be followed by *as* and not *than*.)

✓ *What I want from my life is every bit as important **as**, if not more so than, what John wants.*

✓ (even better) *What I want from my life is every bit as important **as** what John wants, if not more so.*

Cases where the number (singular or plural) changes should also be avoided:

? *The leader was exiled and his followers ∧ imprisoned.* (The word needed before 'imprisoned' is *were*, not *was*.)

✓ *The leader was exiled and his followers **were** imprisoned.*

Apostrophes and possessives

Possessives show possession: *June's email address*; *her mother*. (*June's* and *her* are both possessive words.) The final *-s* preceded by an apostrophe is the typical possessive marker in English. The position of the apostrophe before or after the *-s* can be confusing, but there are fairly simple rules to follow:

• When the noun is singular (i.e. it refers to one person or thing) you form the possessive by adding *-'s*:

the woman's coat (one woman), *the car's windscreen* (one car), *the boss's office* (one boss), *Scotland's historic capital*.

• When the noun is plural (i.e. it refers to more than one person or thing) and ends in *-s*, you form the possessive by adding *-s'*:

the cars' windscreens, the bosses' offices, the Browns' address.

• When the noun is plural and ends in a letter other than *-s*, you form the possessive in the same way as singular nouns, by adding *-'s*:

the women's coats, people's rights.

• When the noun ends in a letter other than *-s*, the apostrophe comes before the added *-s* when it refers to a singular noun (*a boy's mother*) and after it when it refers to more than one (*the three boys' mother*).

Possessives are used to show wider relationships than plain ownership; for example, association and relevance:

*There is a life jacket under **your** seat*. (= the seat you are using)
*I will go and see **my** GP straight away*. (= the GP I am registered with)
*I met **Stephen's** old friend Robert Smith*. (= the friend associated with Stephen)

Possessives ending in *-s* can be a very convenient way of expressing these relationships, but with longer words they can become cumbersome and are best expressed in other ways, typically by using *of*:

? *There are problems in the language's structure*.
✓ *There are problems in the structure of the language*.

Double possessives

Double possessives are constructions of the type *a friend of my brother's* and *an admirer of theirs*, in which the possession is doubly indicated by the word *of* and the possessive forms (*brother's* and *theirs*). This construction is well established and continues alongside the simpler forms *a friend of my brother* and *an admirer of them*. (The emphasis in these types is clearly different, in implying other friends and admirers, from the even simpler *my brother's friend* and *their admirer*.) Sometimes a double possessive usefully avoids ambiguity: for example, *a photograph of my mother* would typically mean a photograph depicting the speaker's mother, whereas *a photograph of my mother's* would mean a photograph (subject unspecified) owned by the mother. But double possessives are not normally used with non-personal nouns such as the names of institutions. So, for example, *a supporter of Manchester United's* would be unidiomatic, and *a supporter of Manchester United* would be the correct form.

The meaning trap: avoiding ambiguity

Sometimes the words we use, and the ways in which we put words together, can also lead to more than one meaning being possible, because the same word can have more than one role or meaning. For example, if someone says to you that you should 'check your speed', this could mean either 'reduce your speed' or 'look and see what your speed is', because the verb *check* has both these key meanings.

This situation, called **ambiguity**, is normally unintentional, although deliberate ambiguity is sometimes found as a literary device or for special effect, e.g. in advertising. In speech, the rise and fall of the voice usually eliminates ambiguity. In writing, the context can make the right meaning clear, but it does not always do so.

Typical types of ambiguity in everyday language usually involve:

• the association of a word or phrase with the wrong part of the sentence in so-called 'misrelated constructions':

? *The Prime Minister was told of the capture of British soldiers while at Leeds watching cricket.*
(It is more likely that the Prime Minister was at Leeds when he was told the news, than that the soldiers were captured there while watching cricket; but even momentary ambiguity is distracting, and it can be avoided in this case by placing *while at Leeds watching cricket* after *told,* or at the beginning of the sentence.)

? *The claims were regarded as mere posturing by the management.*
(Here *by the management* should be placed after *regarded*.)

• the use of a negative with unclear reference, especially in statements of intention or reason:

? *She did not go out just so she could see us.* (Did she go out for some other reason, or stay at home in the hope of seeing us? If it's the second, a comma after *go out* would make this clear.)

• lack of clarity about how far a modifying word applies:

? *The house had a green door and shutters.*

It is not clear whether the doors and shutters were all green or just the doors. Possible alternatives, depending on the meaning, are:

✓ *The house had shutters and a green door.*

or

✓ *The house had a green door and green shutters.*

• words or expressions that have more than one meaning or function:

? *Visiting friends can be tiresome.*
(Even when it is acting as a noun, as *visiting* is here, a verb can take an object, in this case *friends*, so that in this sentence *visiting friends* can either mean a process – 'the activity of going to visit friends' – or a group of people – 'friends who come to visit'.)

Possible solutions are:

✓ *Friends who visit can be tiresome.*
✓ *Going to visit friends can be tiresome.*
✓ *It can be tiresome visiting friends.*
✓ *It can be tiresome having visits from friends.*

And this example:

? *The Minister appealed to her supporters.*

could be resolved into either:

✓ *The Minister made an appeal to her supporters.*

or:

✓ *Her supporters found the Minister appealing.*

• a pronoun with wrong or unclear reference:

? *If your children don't like their toys, get rid of them.*

We hope this means:

✓ *Get rid of the toys your children don't like.*

3
What words mean

'When I use a word,' Humpty Dumpty said, in a rather scornful tone, 'it means just what I choose it to mean – neither more nor less.' 'The question is,' said Alice, 'whether you can make a word mean so many different things.'

Lewis Carroll, *Through the Looking Glass*, 1872

New meanings

Words change their meanings over time. People accept this intellectually, and even applaud it, but they tend to be unsettled by changes when they see them happening within their own experience. This has happened with commonly used words such as *aggravate* (originally 'to make more serious', now often 'to annoy') and *anticipate* (originally 'to forestall', now usually 'to expect'), and can arise when words are confused with other words, as we shall see with *flaunt* (confused with *flout*) and *fortuitous* (confused with *fortunate*). Sometimes older meanings survive alongside newer ones (occasionally causing problems of ambiguity); in other cases the new meanings supersede the older ones. Most interesting of all are those words that lose a meaning and then regain it years later: a case in point is *disinterested*. This used to mean the same as *uninterested*, then developed a special meaning 'impartial', and in recent usage has begun to be used in its older meaning again, to the dismay of the language guardians.

Some words have changed so drastically that they now have virtually the opposite of their original meaning: for example, *nice*. The original meaning of *nice* was 'foolish' or 'stupid'; by various degrees it came to mean 'fine or subtle' as in *a nice distinction* (a meaning it still has), and then 'good or pleasant' (its main current meaning) as in *a nice time, a nice film, a nice holiday*, and anything at all that is welcome or enjoyable. From being a rather unpleasant little word it has gone through so many contortions of meaning that it is now everyone's favourite word for describing things they like.

Words can develop new areas of meaning. For example, *check* has three core meanings: 'to restrain' (*These distractions had the effect of checking our progress*), 'to verify', now the most common (*Before leaving the house he checked that the doors and windows were locked*), and a third meaning, which may now appear to be an incidental one but is in fact the oldest meaning of all: the meaning in chess, 'to threaten an opponent's king' (the word *check* is derived from the Persian word *shah* meaning 'king'). The verb *start* has two core meanings: 'to jump in surprise' (*A noise outside made me start*) and the later meaning 'to begin' (*Work will start next month*). Both meanings remain in current use, and they are sufficiently different to make problems of ambiguity unlikely.

Old meanings

Words have to earn their keep in the language. When a word is no longer needed it will either disappear altogether or acquire a new meaning that is more useful. A case in point is the controversial verb *decimate*. Its original meaning is 'to kill every tenth person' (usually as a military punishment) and is derived from its use in the context of Roman history: *decimus* is the Latin word for 'tenth'. This meaning has largely died out, along with the practice itself, leaving a useful word with nothing much to do. Usage has therefore given it a new meaning, 'to kill in large numbers' (to reduce *to* a tenth instead of *by* a tenth, perhaps), a practice which is as prevalent as ever. This tendency is fuelled by the urge people often have to favour a less familiar (and therefore arguably more powerful) word over a routine word (in this case, *kill*), in the belief that this will make a stronger impression on the reader. At the beginning of this section I observed that people tend to accept meaning change when seen historically but are slower to accept it when it is happening within their own experience; *decimate* is a very good example of this. Eventually the new meaning will be so common as to pass unnoticed, but at the moment it remains controversial. It is most acceptable in contexts involving physical death and destruction:

? *Special help was given to areas that had been decimated by war.*

In figurative meanings that do not involve physical killing or destruction at all its strong resonance makes it much less suitable:

✗ *Under the last government the cab trade had been decimated.*
✗ *Cuts of that level would decimate the existing service.*

Weakened meanings
Adjectives and adverbs

There are two types of adjectives, such as *awful*, *frightful*, and *terrible* on the one hand, and *fabulous*, *incredible*, and *terrific* on the other, which have very strong basic meanings. Those that describe something bad or unpleasant are often based on words denoting powerful feelings or emotions, principally fear (e.g. *dread*, *fright*, *terror*) or suffering (e.g. *chronic*, which refers originally to illness), while those that are favourable in tone are often based on more imaginative or romantic notions (*awe*, *fantasy*, *marvel*):

favourable	*awesome, fabulous, fantastic, incredible, magical, marvellous, sensational, terrific, tremendous*
unfavourable	*abysmal, atrocious, awful, chronic, diabolical, dreadful, frightful, terrible*

Strong words of this kind tend to lose their power with use and develop so-called 'weakened meanings' in everyday contexts, in which the full force of the original meaning is considerably reduced, even to the point of extinction. A *fantastic idea* is more likely to mean 'a very good or interesting idea' than 'an idea based on fantasy' (which is the original meaning of *fantastic*), and *a terrible time* is more likely to mean 'a very unpleasant time' than 'a time of terror' (which is the original meaning of *terrible*). The heavy use these words enjoy in their weakened meanings can compromise their roles in their original meanings. In the examples of weakened uses, the ticked alternatives are much more effective in conveying the meaning:

(weakened) **?** *The challenge for the networks will be whether they can cope with such change and still capture enough of the extra data revenues to justify those **awesome** [✓ huge] licence fees.*
(original) ✓ *Her voice may no longer be in the first flush of youth, but her artistry remains **awesome** [= causing wonder].*

(weakened) **?** *I think it is **diabolical** [✓ deplorable] that we have a French company taking British contracts for London Underground and giving it to Spanish workers.*
(original) ✓ *When researchers watched these bats in their daytime roosts, they couldn't quite believe what they were seeing, for in a protracted afternoon ritual the bats concocted a mixture more **diabolical** than anything Shakespeare could ever have imagined.*

(weakened) **?** *What he has achieved is **incredible** [✓ outstanding or exceptional] and the way he has gone about it is **fantastic** [✓ admirable or exemplary].*
(original) ✓ *There is a **fantastic** intensity and wildness, almost savagery, in the landscapes of Spain.*

In the last example, *fantastic* is used in its full meaning: the landscape is described in terms of fantasy. But it will probably be understood as meaning 'interesting' or 'exciting', which is only part of the intended meaning. If there is any doubt about your real meaning being misunderstood, it is better to use other words that do not involve this kind of uncertainty, such as *bizarre, fanciful,* or *imaginative*; even a simpler word like *strange* can be much more effective:

✓ *There is a strange intensity and wildness, almost savagery, in the landscapes of Spain.*

The adverbs based on these words (*awfully, dreadfully, fantastically, incredibly, terribly,* etc.) have weakened even further in meaning to little more than 'very' or 'extremely':

? *Something has been happening, and it's something **dreadfully** annoying.*

? *It wasn't until I saw the reviews and the reactions of the audiences that I realized there were bits that people found **incredibly** touching.*

? *When I told Keith he was **terribly** upset and left me.*

The result of all this meaning dilution is that words of this kind tend to become sentence-fillers lacking real effect. They have a useful role in adding colour to every-day conversation, and it would be difficult to avoid them totally. But if you want your writing to show genuine conviction, it is best to use other words that still make an impact, such as *excellent, remarkable, spectacular, outstanding, exceptional, extraordinary, momentous,* or *phenomenal.*

As regards intensifying adverbs, a simpler word such as *extremely, exceedingly, exceptionally* (or sometimes, as with feelings, *intensely* or *acutely*) will often be more effective:

✓ *It wasn't until I saw the reviews and the reactions of the audiences that I realized there were bits that people found extremely* [or *intensely*] *touching.*

Special mention is needed of *awful* and *awfully*, because these words have gone furthest along the road of weakened meaning and have ended up as catch-all intensifiers, as in *an awful shame* or *awfully good*. In this meaning the tone is very informal, more suited to conversation than to formal writing. It is a favourite stand-by of journalists writing for a mass market:

? *So if we are serious about drawing the line between private and public, there is an* **awful** *lot [✓ a large quantity or a great deal] of toothpaste to be put back into rather a lot of tubes.*

? *We have people in our projects who have been on the streets an* **awfully** *[✓ a very] long time.*

Nouns

Some nouns that have special or semi-technical meanings, such as *dilemma* and *alibi*, tend to develop more generalized meanings that compromise the main meaning. Strictly speaking, a *dilemma* is a difficult choice or predicament involving two possibilities, both of them unfavourable:

✓ *It was a way of easing the* **dilemma** *of choosing between cutting public services and increasing taxes.*

Do not use *dilemma* if you simply mean 'problem' or 'difficulty':

✗ *The control of junior staff is an enduring* **dilemma** *for bureaucracies.*

An *alibi* is a legal term for evidence of where an accused person was at the time of a crime:

✓ *Luckily we've both got a very good **alibi** for last night.*

Do not use *alibi* if you simply mean 'excuse' or 'pretext':

✗ *Management is provided with an **alibi** for poor performance by the constant ministerial interference.*

The table below shows other words that have controversial meanings and need care in use. Some of them are explained in more detail, with examples of use, in the **Hitlist** in section 5.

word	main meaning	controversial meaning
aggravate	to make worse	to annoy
alibi	evidence that a person was elsewhere	an excuse or pretext
anticipate	to forestall or prevent	to expect
cohort	a group of people	a companion
crescendo	an increasing noise or excitement	a climax
decimate	to kill one in ten of	to kill or destroy a large proportion of
dilemma	a difficult choice between two or more alternatives	a problem
enormity	an act of great wickedness	great size
feasible	able to be done or carried out	likely or probable

word	main meaning	controversial meaning
fulsome	excessive; cloying and insincere (as in *fulsome praise*)	extravagant (in favourable senses)
ironic	showing irony	strange, paradoxical
majority	the larger or largest number (as in *the majority of people*)	the largest part (as in *the majority of the money*)
mutual	shown by each towards the other (as in *mutual respect*)	shared (as in *a mutual friend*)
pristine	in its original condition	completely clean, spotless
transpire	to come to be known, to emerge	to happen

Confused meanings

Some words with different meanings are commonly confused, usually because their forms are close. Often one of the confused words is substitutable for the other in a way that still produces good sense, although it is not the sense intended. A good example is *fortuitous*, which does not mean 'fortunate' but 'coincidental' (as in *our meeting was fortuitous*: it happened by chance). *Regrettable* means 'to be regretted' (as in *their inter-vention was regrettable*) and *regretful* means 'having regrets' (as in *she shook her head with a regretful smile*); they are often confused especially in their adverb forms *regrettably* and *regretfully*. *Prevaricate* means 'to be evasive' and *procrastinate* means 'to put off action', meanings that are close enough to enable confusion between them to go unnoticed by the reader, although their precise meanings are different.

Some words overlap significantly in one meaning, but should be carefully distinguished in others. For example, *doubtful* and *dubious* are interchangeable in the meanings 'causing doubt' and 'uncertain':

It is a doubtful/dubious theory at best.
I was doubtful/dubious about the outcome.

But in the meaning 'unconvinced' (applied to a person), *doubtful* and not *dubious* should be used:

*She had a **doubtful** look on her face.*

Doubtful can be followed by *that* or *whether*, whereas *dubious* cannot:

*We are **doubtful** whether this idea will work.*

But in the meaning 'open to question, of questionable value or worth', *dubious* and not *doubtful* is the choice:

*The appeal was rejected on **dubious** grounds.*

Other pairs of words have meanings that overlap considerably, but there is a distinction in their application: for example, *forceful* and *forcible* are often interchangeable, but *forcible* is not used about a person whereas *forceful* is.

The table below lists words with meanings that are often confused. In some cases you will find more information about them in the **Hitlist** in section 5, which also includes other cases (such as *partially* and *partly*) that are too complex to summarize here.

word 1	wordclass	meaning	word 2	meaning
adherence	noun	following the rules, a belief, etc.	adhesion	the act of sticking
adjacent	adjective	nearby without necessarily joining (as in *they sat at adjacent tables*)	adjoining	next to and touching (as in *adjoining rooms*)
admission	noun	an acknowledgement; the right to enter	admittance	permission to enter
adverse	adjective	contrary (wind); unfavourable	averse	strongly opposed
affect	verb	to produce a change in	effect (verb)	to cause or bring about
			effect (noun)	the result of a cause
allusion	noun	an implied or indirect reference	illusion	a false impression or appearance
alternate	adjective	occurring one after another	alternative	providing another possibility
alternate	verb	to interchange		
ambiguous	adjective	having more than one possible meaning	ambivalent	uncertain in feeling or attitude
amend	verb	to correct or revise	emend	to alter or correct (a text)

word 1	wordclass	meaning	word 2	meaning
amoral	adjective	having no moral sense or understanding	*immoral*	not conforming to accepted moral standards
appraise	verb	to assess the worth or importance of	*apprise*	to inform about something
authoritarian	adjective	(said of a person) dictatorial or domineering	*authoritative*	(said of opinions or writings) recognized as dependable
avoid	verb	to keep away from or shun	*evade*	to avoid by skill or deception
biannual	adjective	occurring twice a year	*biennial*	occurring every two years
censor	verb	to remove material from a film, play, etc.	*censure*	to fault or criticize
ceremonial	adjective	with ritual or ceremony (neutral in meaning: *ceremonial dress*)	*ceremonious*	devoted to form and ceremony; punctilious (judgmental in meaning)
childish	adjective	immature like a child (unfavourable, e.g. *childish behaviour*)	*childlike*	innocent like a child (favourable, e.g. *with childlike enthusiasm*)
classic	adjective	recognized as typical or outstanding (as in *the classic book on the subject, a classic remark of his*)	*classical*	to do with the ancient world of Greece and Rome; to do with serious or conventional music

word 1	wordclass	meaning	word 2	meaning
climactic	adjective	causing or forming a climax	*climatic*	to do with climate
coherent	adjective	logically clear and consistent	*cohesive*	sticking well; united
complacent	adjective	uncritically pleased with oneself	*complaisant*	inclined to please
compose	verb	(said of parts) to constitute or make up a whole	*comprise*	(said of a whole) to consist of parts
condole	verb	to express sympathy or sorrow	*console*	to comfort
consequent	adjective	(with *on*) resulting from or following on from	*consequential*	resulting (as in *consequential changes*); significant
contemptible	adjective	deserving contempt	*contemptuous*	showing contempt
continual	adjective	recurring repeatedly	*continuous*	continuing without interruption
credible	adjective	reasonable enough to believe	*credulous*	too ready to believe
creditable	adjective	deserving praise or acknowledgement	*credible*	reasonable enough to believe
decided	adjective	clear and unquestionable (a *decided victory* is indisputable in itself)	*decisive*	*of crucial importance; conclusive (a decisive victory is important in its consequences)*

word 1	wordclass	meaning	word 2	meaning
defective	adjective	having a fault or defect	*deficient*	having a lack or deficiency
defuse	verb	to remove the fuse from, to make less dangerous or tense	*diffuse* (adjective)	scattered; not concisely expressed
definite	adjective	free of uncertainty; clear and distinct	*definitive*	authoritative and exhaustive
deprecate	verb	to express disapproval of	*depreciate*	to lower in value; to belittle
discomfit	verb	to cause embarrassment or uncertainty in	*discomfort*	to make uneasy
discreet	adjective	cautious and modest in what one says	*discrete*	separate, distinct (as in *two discrete stages in the process*)
disinterested	adjective	impartial; lacking selfish motives	*uninterested*	not interested
distinct	adjective	separate, different (as in *a word with several distinct meanings*); definite or obvious (*a distinct possibility*)	*distinctive*	characteristic and helping to identify (*his characteristic laugh*)
doubtful	adjective	having or showing doubt	*dubious*	causing doubt; suspect

word 1	wordclass	meaning	word 2	meaning
eatable	adjective	fit for eating, pleasant to eat (as in *the rest of the meal was barely eatable*)	*edible*	suitable to eat, not poisonous (as in *edible mushrooms*)
effective	adjective	having the right effect	*effectual*	capable of producing the right effect
emotional	adjective	to do with or affected by the emotions; showing emotion	*emotive*	causing emotion (as in *an emotive issue*)
enormity	noun	a grave crime or wicked act	*enormousness*	large size or scale
ensure	verb	to make sure	*insure*	to take out insurance on
equable	adjective	even and regular (*an equable temper, an equable climate*)	*equitable*	fair and just (*equitable treatment*)
especially	adverb	above all; very much	*specially*	for a special reason or purpose
euphemism	noun	a mild or indirect term used instead of an unpleasant or offensive one	*euphuism*	an artificially ornate style of writing
exalt	verb	to praise highly	*exult*	to rejoice openly
exceptionable	adjective	likely to cause objection	*exceptional*	unusual; superior
exhausting	adjective	extremely tiring	*exhaustive*	comprehensive, thorough

word 1	wordclass	meaning	word 2	meaning
factious	adjective	causing or involving conflict (as in *factious quarrelling*)	*fractious*	irritable and restless (as in *a fractious child*)
fatal	adjective	causing death or bringing ruin (as in *a fatal blow*, *a fatal effect*)	*fateful*	having decisive or far-reaching consequences (as in *a fateful turn of events*)
fearful	adjective	full of fear; unpleasant	*fearsome*	appalling or frightening (usually in appearance)
flaunt	verb	to display ostentatiously	*flout*	to disregard rules or treat them with contempt
flounder	verb	(said of a person) to act or speak in a confused way	*founder*	(said of an undertaking) to fail or collapse
forbear	verb	to hold back from	*forbear* (noun)	an ancestor
forceful	adjective	strong and vigorous (*a forceful blow*); possessing force or strength (*a forceful personality*)	*forcible*	done with great force, usually against resistance
fortuitous	adjective	occurring by chance; coincidental	*fortunate*	occurring by good chance, lucky

word 1	wordclass	meaning	word 2	meaning
gourmand	noun	a glutton	*gourmet*	a connoisseur of food
homogeneous	adjective	of the same kind; uniform	*homogenous*	having common descent
illegal	adjective	against the law	*illicit*	not allowed
immunity	noun	freedom from a disease; freedom from something unpleasant	*impunity*	exemption from or avoidance of punishment
imperial	adjective	to do with empire or an emperor	*imperious*	domineering
imply	verb	to express indirectly or suggest	*infer*	to deduce or conclude
impracticable	adjective	not able to be done or carried out; not feasible	*impractical*	not practical or realistic
inapt	adjective	not suitable	*inept*	clumsy or incompetent
incredible	adjective	too improbable to be believed	*incredulous*	unable or unwilling to believe
ingenious	adjective	clever; well thought out	*ingenuous*	innocent and open; honest
insidious	adjective	proceeding quietly and harmfully (as in *insidious forms of discrimination*)	*invidious*	causing resentment (as in *invidious to single out names*)

word 1	wordclass	meaning	word 2	meaning
intense	adjective	extreme in force or degree; feeling emotion deeply	*intensive*	highly concentrated; thorough
interment	noun	the burial of a corpse	*internment*	confinement in prison in wartime
judicial	adjective	relating to legal justice	*judicious*	showing sound judgment
junction	noun	a point where things are joined, especially roads and railway lines	*juncture*	a critical or dramatic moment (usually *at this juncture*)
loose	adjective and verb	not fixed; to untie or make less tight	*lose* (verb)	to suffer the loss of or no longer have
luxuriant	adjective	(said mainly of growing things) lush; abundant	*luxurious*	comfortable and of high quality
masterful	adjective	inclined to take control or dominate	*masterly*	showing great skill or expertise
mendacity	noun	habitual lying	*mendicity*	begging
meretricious	adjective	showy and false	*meritorious*	commendable; worthy of merit
militate	verb	to have force or effect against (e.g. *these difficulties militate against an early solution*)	*mitigate*	to make less harsh or hostile

word 1	wordclass	meaning	word 2	meaning
nationalize	verb	to take an industry into state ownership	*naturalize*	to grant citizenship to a foreigner
observance	noun	the keeping of a law or custom, etc.	*observation*	perception; a remark
obsolescent	adjective	going out of use	*obsolete*	outdated and no longer used
occupant	noun	a person in a vehicle, etc.	*occupier*	the owner or tenant of a property
official	adjective	approved by authority	*officious*	unpleasantly zealous in asserting authority
peaceable	adjective	disposed to prefer peace (as in *a peaceable nation*)	*peaceful*	characterized by peace; tranquil
permissible	adjective	allowed	*permissive*	morally tolerant
perquisite	noun	a special right or privilege that goes with a job or position	*prerequisite*	something needed in advance
perspicacious	adjective	mentally acute or perceptive	*perspicuous*	clear and understandable
pitiable	adjective	deserving or arousing pity (generally sympathetic)	*pitiful*	causing pity or commiseration; contemptible (as in *a pitiful excuse*)

word 1	wordclass	meaning	word 2	meaning
practicable	adjective	able to be done or carried out; feasible	*practical*	effective or realistic; (said of a person) skilled at manual tasks
precipitate	adjective	acting or done very suddenly	*precipitous*	dangerously steep or high
prescribe	verb	to recommend or instruct with authority; to issue a medical prescription	*proscribe*	to condemn or prohibit
prevaricate	verb	to speak or act evasively	*procrastinate*	to put off doing something
purposely	adverb	with an express purpose; intentionally	*purposefully*	with determination
rebound	verb	to have a harmful effect on the originator (with *on*: *these slanders will rebound on them*)	*redound*	to contribute favourably to (with *to*: *it can only redound to our advantage*)
refute	verb	to prove to be wrong by argument or evidence	*repudiate*	to reject as untrue; to disown
regrettably	adverb	in a way that is regretted; not as one would wish	*regretfully*	with a feeling of regret
seasonable	adjective	suitable for the time (as in *seasonable attire*)	*seasonal*	associated with a particular time of year (as in *seasonal rainfall*)

word 1	wordclass	meaning	word 2	meaning
sensual	adjective	to do with sexual gratification of the body	*sensuous*	gratifying or appealing to the senses (rather than the intellect)
sociable	adjective	friendly and wanting to mix with people	*social*	to do with human society
titillate	verb	to excite or arouse pleasantly	*titivate*	to adorn or smarten
tortuous	adjective	twisting and bendy; devious	*torturous*	causing suffering; tormenting
triumphal	adjective	done or put up in celebration of a victory (as in *triumphal arch*)	*triumphant*	jubilant after a victory or success
unsociable	adjective	reserved and reluctant to mix with people	*unsocial*	socially awkward (as in *unsocial hours*)
venal	adjective	open to bribery; corrupt	*venial*	(said of a sin) minor
veracity	noun	truth (as in *the veracity of the statement*)	*voracity*	greed
waive	verb	to forgo a right	*wave*	to signal with the arm

Saying too much: tautology

Tautology, from Greek words meaning 'same' and 'word', is a form of word redundancy in which the same idea or meaning is expressed more than once in a phrase or sentence, as in *a free gift* (all gifts are free), *a new innovation*, and *to repeat again*. Some tautologies are contained within a small group of words such as a noun phrase (e.g. *future prospects, past history, no other alternative, the general consensus*). This kind of tautology is common, especially in the rapid flow of speech, and some have become idiomatic (such as *free gift* and *past history*).

Other tautologies occur in the way sentences are put together, and involve redundant words that can be removed from the writing without in any way diluting or compromising the meaning (in these examples the tautologies are in bold):

✗ *Back payments of income support were to be limited **only** to a three-year period.*
✗ *There is no need for **undue** haste.*
✗ *The Cold War came to a **final** close in Germany yesterday.*

In each sentence the words shown can be omitted without any loss of sense because their meanings are contained in other words.

Putting it nicely: euphemism

Euphemism is the use of a milder or vaguer word or expression in place of one that might seem too harsh or direct. It is a social phenomenon as much as a linguistic one because it is used with regard to people's (assumed) sensitivities. The most productive subjects for euphemism are bodily functions (*to be excused, to relieve oneself*), sexual activity (*to make love, to sleep together, a fallen woman*), nakedness (*in one's birthday suit, in a state of nature*), parentage and illegitimacy (*love child, wrong side of the blanket*), old age (*senior citizen, sunset years*), death (*to pass away, to face one's maker*), politics and international relations (*fifth column, full and frank discussions, internal security, population transfer*), employment and economic life (*negative equity, jobseeker, downsizing, headcount reduction, regrouping, to dispense with someone's services*), and violence (*to do away, to eliminate, to wipe out*).

There are times when this kind of softening of reality is needed to avoid offence or embarrassment. But there are two kinds of euphemisms that can be unwelcome or even offensive:

• those that obscure or generalize the meaning (e.g. *sexual assault* for *rape*) or cause misunderstanding (e.g. *cloakroom* for *lavatory*).
• those that attempt to make repellent or destructive activities appear harmless or constructive (e.g. *ethnic cleansing* and *population transfer* for the wholesale killing or deportation of peoples, *collateral damage* for the accidental destruction of non-military areas in war, and *surgical strike* for a bombing raid).

Some euphemisms have become bureaucratic clichés and are best avoided in general use, e.g. *helping the police with their inquiries* ('under interrogation and about to be charged') and *exploring every avenue* ('making extensive inquiries'). Others are only suitable in humorous contexts, e.g. *tired and emotional* ('drunk') and *economical with the truth* ('lying').

In other words: synonyms and antonyms

Synonyms are words that are identical or close in meaning, such as the pair *close* and *shut*, or the trio *begin*, *start*, and *commence*. In the core vocabulary of English this often came about because words came into English from other languages, especially Old Norse during the Viking raids of the ninth and tenth centuries and French after the Norman Conquest in 1066, and failed to drive out those already in use. For example, *close* is a Middle English (13th century) word derived from Old French, and joined the existing Old English word *shut*. Because French was the language of government in England after the Norman Conquest, some of the words taken from French belong to the world of administration and officialdom and sound affected or pretentious in ordinary use, e.g. *commence* instead of *begin*, or *purchase* instead of *buy*.

Other pairs of words have their own special areas of use; for example, *kill* is a general word whereas *slay* is literary or rhetorical, and *little* implies an affection or intimacy that is not present in the more neutral word *small* (compare *a little child* and *a small child*). *Baby* is a general word for a newborn child, *infant* has a special meaning, and *neonate* is used only in medical contexts.

There are few words with meanings that are exactly the same, in the sense that they can be used interchangeably with no effect on the overall meaning. Most synonyms that you find in a list in a thesaurus are close rather than identical in meaning, and they are not always used in identical ways. Take, for example, the three words *accuse*, *blame*, and *charge*. You accuse someone *of* a wrong, blame someone *for* a wrong, and charge someone *with* a wrong. The words *danger* and *risk* have close meanings, and can be substituted for each other in some sentences:

✓ *There was a danger of meeting floods on the road.*
✓ *There was a risk of meeting floods on the road.*

But there are important differences of usage. For example, you describe a person or thing as being *in danger* but *at risk*; *in danger* is used with physical as well as situational reference whereas *at risk* is more usually situational; and *in danger* can be reversed as *out of danger* whereas *at risk* can only be made negative by adding *not*.

✓ *She was now out of danger and would soon return home.*
✗ *She was now out of risk and would soon return home.*

✓ *The employees' pension rights were now at risk.*
✗ *The employees' pension rights were now at danger.*

Other synonyms are more restricted in use than the words they replace. For example, *inform* and *instruct* are given as synonyms of different senses of *tell*, but their effect is more formal:

✓ *Will you tell them to come here?*
✓ *Will you instruct them to come here?*

✓ *A police officer told her that her husband had been injured in an accident.*
✓ *A police officer informed her that her husband had been injured in an accident.*

In the first pair, *tell* is the more natural choice, whereas the more official nature of the second pair makes *inform* more suitable. The information given in larger dictionaries can help you here, if your intuitions need support, because they add labels (such as *formal*, *informal*, and *archaic*) that tell you about the appropriateness of words to particular styles of speaking or writing.

Some words have synonyms that are really euphemisms, or ways of saying something unpleasant in a more pleasant way (see above), such as *pass away* or *perish* for *die*. You need to be careful when you use synonyms of this type as the effect can sometimes be artificial and coy.

Other synonyms are not really equivalents at all but are special kinds of a more general word. There is no synonym for the word *bed* (in its furniture meaning): words like *berth, bunk, divan*, and *futon* are not alternatives for the word *bed* but types of bed, and you can only use them when you mean that particular type (and even then you will be changing the emphasis). There is no synonym for *sing*: words like *chant, croon*, and *warble* mean particular kinds of singing but not singing in general.

The best place to look for synonyms is in a thesaurus, which organizes words in groups having the same meaning. Some thesauruses, notably Roget's, are completely thematic in that the headings that synonyms are put under are structured groups of ideas and topics (such as life and death, the human body, movement, etc.), but most thesauruses are arranged alphabetically under keywords as in a conventional dictionary, with lists of synonyms (preferably listed in order of usefulness and not in alphabetical order, which is arbitrary in terms of meaning) in place of definitions.

The most useful synonyms are those that can be substituted as more exact or descriptive alternatives for very general high-level words. The following sentences all contain the adjective *nice*, which is one of the most overworked words in English:

*We had a very **nice** apartment in Bloomsbury.*
*We are hoping it will be **nice** tomorrow.*
*It's a very **nice** piece of work.*
*The flask was handed over to a **nice** woman, who filled it with soup.*
*It was **nice** of them to say that.*

In ordinary conversation *nice* will often be adequate in these sentences, but in more continuous speaking and writing it is useful to find alternatives to avoid constant repetition of the same much-used word. Anyone hearing or reading the word *nice* over and over again is likely to become tired of it. Alternatives to *nice* in the five sentences above are as follows (some synonyms, e.g. *pleasant*, apply to several senses):

We had a very comfortable [or agreeable or pleasant] apartment in Bloomsbury.
We are hoping it will be fine (or sunny or warm or pleasant) tomorrow.
It's a very fine [or good or pleasing] piece of work.
The flask was handed over to a likeable [or kind or generous or pleasant] woman, who filled it with soup.
It was kind [or generous or considerate or helpful] of them to say that.

Notice that *pleasant* is possible in three of these sentences. It is often an improvement on *nice* but because it too is so wide in meaning it is liable to be overused in the same way as *nice* is.

Antonyms are words that are opposite in meaning, such as *push* and *pull*, and *give* and *take*. There are few genuine antonyms in language, because few words allow opposite meaning (even *give* and *take* are only approximately opposite in some contexts). Some words do not have any genuine antonyms. Most nouns for specific physical objects such as *bed* and *floor* cannot have opposites (*ceiling* is not an opposite of *floor* but a counterpart in the real world), nor can classifying words such as *triangular* and *Flemish*. The verb *have* has many meanings but the antonyms sometimes adduced for it (such as *lack* and *lose*) are complementary processes or states rather than genuine opposites.

Adding a touch of colour: figures of speech

Figures of speech are special uses of words that help to make language more interesting and colourful. They typically involve substituting a more powerful or vivid word or phrase for an ordinary one, in order to provide the reader with a stronger image than normal language can offer:

Whenever he had nothing better to do, he would sink into sleep. Sleep devoured boredom. Sleep devoured time.

This sentence is about a soldier in a camp in Egypt during a hot afternoon. The writer could have said, more simply, that he *went to sleep to pass the time*. But the physical language of sinking into sleep and time being eaten up enriches the meaning and presents the reader with a powerful image of inactivity from the real world that conveys the meaning much more effectively.

Devices like these are not limited to the realms of fiction and creative writing. We constantly use them in everyday language. When we talk about the *eye* of a storm, a *sheet* of lightning, *music* to our ears, or plans bearing *fruit*, we are not referring to an eye in its literal meaning, nor to an actual sheet, nor to real music or edible fruit. These so-called 'figurative' meanings are figures of speech as much as the *sinking into sleep* in the literary example above. They allow the basic stock of vocabulary to take on new layers of meaning that effectively double its usefulness, as well as enriching the language by producing interesting or attractive mental images.

Many idioms and fixed expressions that we use regularly in everyday language are also miniature figures of speech using images based on metaphor: *once in a blue moon, have one's head in the clouds, till the cows come home, pull someone's leg, be round the bend, get down to brass tacks, turn over a new leaf.*

Comparisons: similes and metaphors

The most common figures of speech in ordinary language are comparisons called similes and metaphors. A **simile** (pronounced **sim**-i-li, from the Latin word *similis* meaning 'like') is a comparison that is spoken or spelled out explicitly, usually with the words *as* or *like*. Here are some examples:

*The river was well over its banks, and flowing **like an express train**.*
*She shot out of her chair **like a rocket**.*
*I sat **as still as cold wax**, watching the grey river slug by.*
*You'd have to be **as small as a fig wasp** to get through that hole.*
*Conrad was on the attack **like a crazed bird** beating a cuckoo out of its nest.*

Everyday English is full of idioms that are similes established by usage (although in some the association is not obvious): *as bold as brass, fit as a fiddle, to run like the wind, to sell like hot cakes.*

A **metaphor** (from the Greek word *metaphora* meaning 'transfer' or 'substitution') goes an important stage further and says that the person or thing actually *is* what they are being compared to, so that instead of:

Conrad was on the attack like a crazed bird.

we have:

Conrad was a crazed bird on the attack.

Sometimes there is a thin line dividing simile and metaphor:

(simile) *He said I was behaving like a child.*
(metaphor) *He said what a child I was being.*
(simile) *The music is like a vast cathedral of sound.*
(metaphor) *The music forms a vast cathedral of sound.*

Many proverbs are types of extended metaphor: *a stitch in time saves nine, if the cap fits wear it, look before you leap.*

Mixed metaphor

Because a metaphor is based on a very specific image, you need to be careful when you continue with what you are saying, to avoid introducing another metaphor that clashes with the first. The effect of this can often be comic or absurd. This is not ungrammatical but it can be distracting and is poor style:

After a while Rostov found that he was losing track of the ebb and flow of the conversation.
(*Losing track* presents an image of roads and railways whereas the notion of *ebb and flow* belongs to water and tides.)
He has been made a sacrificial lamb for taking the lid off a can of worms.

You should also avoid a mixture of metaphors and idioms that are incongruous or counter-intuitive when occurring together:

A new version of the program has appeared – hopefully with all the bugs ironed out.
We will take concrete steps to appease the grass roots.

It is easy to fall into this trap in ordinary conversation, but you should take care in writing, when there is more time to think about what you are saying.

On the other hand you should not be fussy about figurative uses. To a great extent, figurative meanings have a life of their own and cannot be made to conform too rigidly to their physical counterparts. Pedantic insistence on origins can bring language to a halt. There is nothing wrong with *increasing targets* (= 'objectives'), even though strictly speaking a larger target in the physical sense is easier to reach and not harder;

nor with *reducing ceilings* (= 'limits, especially on spending') although in its physical form the notion is impossible.

Changing the name: metonymy and synecdoche

Metonymy (pronounced mi-**ton**-i-mi, from the Greek word *metonumia* meaning 'change of name') is another kind of word substitution, by which you can refer to an important or well-known person or institution by something it is closely associated with, e.g. the American presidency is called *the White House*, the British monarchy is called *the Crown*, and Arsenal Football Club is represented by its London ground, *Highbury*. In the proverb *the pen is mightier than the sword*, the word *pen* stands for writing or literature and the word *sword* stands for fighting or warfare.

Synecdoche (pronounced si-**nek**-di-ki, from Greek words meaning 'to take together') is a similar idea that uses a broader term in place of a narrower or less inclusive one, or vice versa, as in *Australia* [= the Australian team] *came out to bat*, *a fleet of fifty sails* (= 'ships'), and *a thousand head* [= animals] *of cattle*. Americans often refer to Britain as *England*, and in doing so they are using a form of synecdoche, although this explanation will not satisfy the people of Scotland, Wales, and Northern Ireland.

Not saying what you mean: irony

Irony (from the Greek word *eironeia* meaning 'pretended ignorance') means several things. In everyday language it refers to the practice of saying something by using words that are the opposite of what you really mean. This creates a special effect and is often more striking than saying what you mean directly. When you look out of the window at the pouring rain and exclaim '*What a lovely day!*', you are using a form of irony. To make your point clear, you would normally use a special tone of voice with more sarcasm than if you were speaking literally.

Irony has other meanings in literature and drama. We are less concerned with these here, but you might come across them. These are:

• *dramatic irony*, in which the audience knows something that the characters on stage or in a film do not.
• *Socratic irony* (after the Greek philosopher Socrates, who used it), in which a participant in a discussion feigns ignorance on a matter so as to lead the others on to admit more than they would otherwise and to lay themselves open to a more effective challenge.

Understating it: meiosis and litotes

Understatement is substituting a weak term or description for a stronger one. As a figure of speech it is called **meiosis** (pronounced my-**oh**-sis, from a Greek word meaning 'lessening'), and it is common in ordinary speech and writing, as when we call a wound 'just a scratch' or a setback 'a minor glitch'. Typically we use this kind of device for social rather than stylistic reasons, especially to spare a hearer's feelings or because the truth directly told might be unwelcome or distressing. Language comes to our aid, and enables us to say something other than what we really mean while still conveying the intended meaning.

There is a special form of meiosis, called **litotes** (pronounced lie-**toe**-teez, from a Greek word *litos* meaning 'plain' or 'meagre'), in which a positive statement is replaced by a negative form of its opposite, which can make the point much more striking:

*I **wasn't** sorry to have missed such a noisy occasion.*
*She spent a lot of time lying on the sofa, but that's **hardly unusual** for a woman of her age and circumstances.*
*Moving 12 million-odd pictures to new premises is **no mean** feat.*
*Turner **never ceased** to observe and comment on nature.*

Overstating it: hyperbole

Hyperbole (pronounced hie-**per**-bi-li, from a Greek word meaning 'throwing beyond') is the opposite of litotes and understatement: it is a form of exaggeration in which a strong term or description is substituted for a weaker one. It is not meant to be taken literally but creates an extreme effect:

I have asked myself this question a thousand times and I still don't have the answer.
Edward closed his eyes and remembered those golden summers now an eternity away.

Some everyday idioms are based on exaggeration and are therefore a kind of ready-made hyperbole: *floods of complaints, loads of time, up to one's ears in work, light years away.*

Shared words: zeugma and syllepsis

Zeugma (pronounced **zyoog**-ma, from a Greek word for 'yoking') is a figure of speech in which a word, or a particular form of a word, is shared by two parts of the sentence but is strictly correct only in one:

Kat was up early and her sisters still in bed. (*Was* fits with *Kat* but not with *her sisters.*)

She's a lovely, intelligent, sensitive woman who has and continues to turn around my life in a wonderfully positive way. (*To turn* fits with *continues* but not with *has.*)

Beware of constructions of this type, which are technically ungrammatical. They are common in everyday conversation but you should avoid them in writing except for special effect.

In another form of zeugma (also called **syllepsis**, pronounced si-**lep**-sis, from a Greek word meaning 'taking together') the 'shared' word fits both contexts grammatically but has different meanings:

He managed to catch his train, his coat in the door, and a heavy cold. (The shared word is *catch.*)

Syllepsis is more acceptable than zeugma because it is formally correct, and sometimes the shared word is repeated for special effect:

Sir Geoffrey Howe, who had arrived in a limousine, the editor of the Daily Telegraph, who had arrived in a motor-boat, and Dave Nellist, who had arrived in an anorak. (The shared word is *in.*)

4

The social side of language

Finding the right level

Writing differs markedly from speech in one very important respect: when you speak you are present and you can add intonation and movement (so-called 'body language') to add meaning and nuance to what you are saying. You are also able to see your listener's reactions and correct any false impressions you may inadvertently give. But when you write your words down, they become separated from you and have to speak entirely for themselves. So it is very important to have a clear perception of who you are writing for, and to take into account their needs and the ways in which they are likely to respond to what you write. You would not write in the same way if you were addressing a child, for example, as if you were writing for an adult. The things you need to take into account are:

- the age of your readers
- their level of education

- the subject you are writing about
- the type of document you are writing.

It is also important to maintain the same style through-out and not switch suddenly. Here is an example taken from a fairly up-market magazine on classical music which aims at writing in an authoritative but relaxed style appropriate to a general readership. For most of the paragraph it is successful, but the reader is pulled up short at the end of the second sentence by the use of a colloquialism (very informal expression) that is unexceptionable in itself but totally out of keeping with what has gone before. Another colloquialism a few words further on also jars, though less so:

*Symphonies written before 1960 by women are relatively rare. There are numerous socio-historical reasons for this: society's narrow expectations for women and their limited education, **for starters** [better: to begin with]. Women rarely got the relevant **hands-on** [better: direct or active or personal] experience of working with an orchestra, let alone the years of intensive compositional training that their male counterparts enjoyed.*

Choice of vocabulary is an important aspect of choos-ing the right style. We are often presented with a range of possible words when we want to express a particular idea. The three words *begin*, *start*, and *commence* all mean much the same, but they can have a different effect in the context of a written statement (not to mention *activate*, *initiate*, *inaugurate*, and other special words). *Little* and *small*, and *big* and *large*, are pairs of synonyms (words having the same meaning) but the connotations are different: *little* and *big* are more emotive or affectionate, whereas *small* and *large* are more neutral in tone. Watch out for these in your reading and notice the different effect they have. Of course, there are many other synonyms for *big* and *small*, which you can readily find in a thesaurus: for *big*, for example, we have a wide choice between *huge, enormous, vast, colossal, gigantic, mountainous*, etc., as well as various informal and humorous words like *mega* and *ginormous*.

There are words that we tend to use only rarely, such as *rebarbative* (meaning 'repellent') and *coexistence* (meaning 'existing or living at the same time'), and we need to be sure that we are using them correctly and effectively. Some words are used in print, and even in speech, as a means of avoiding the supposedly banal or commonplace, where the commonplace is the word needed: *purchase* for *buy* and *edifice* for *building* fall into this category. The effect is of self-conscious mannerism and their use is usually counterproductive. Do not be afraid to use the ordinary word.

A common language sensitivity these days is the use of euphemisms, words and expressions that avoid directly referring to unpleasant or taboo subjects, e.g. *pass away* for *die* and *jobseekers* for *unemployed*. (See pp. 161–2 for more on this.) In business, if a company wants to make staff redundant, they will use terms like *downsizing* and *regrouping*, and tell individuals that *their services are no longer required*. In world affairs, politicians often refer to *the international community* when they are seeking support for a controversial action or policy. This is a vague and roundabout way of including an apparently large number of people without having to specify them in any way. To many people, this is a kind of evasion: using language to obscure the meaning or conceal a lack of real meaning.

As well as formal errors in grammar and usage, there are certain language sensitivities that you need to be aware of if you want to write well and effectively. Some of these sensitivities are linguistic: avoiding clichés for example, and language features that are not necessarily wrong in a formal sense but offend people and therefore put them off what you are trying to say in your writing. We have noted these in previous sections, where it was shown that some of them are superstitions: the split infinitive is the most common of these; insistence on *different from* is another. But even if they are superstitions and are not based on identifiable language principles, they are an aspect of language use that everyone needs to be aware of.

Other sensitivities are not really about language and grammar as such but are based on social considerations and are to do with the effect particular words and expressions might have on people: avoiding words that offend, for example, or that can have pejorative meanings. Sex-specific words such as *policeman* and *chairman* have given way to more inclusive alternatives such as *police officer* and *chairperson*, and you can use *synthetic* or *manufactured* instead of the more gender-specific *man-made* and *human resources* instead of *manpower*. Idioms that are heavily dependent on gender, such as *every man for himself*, are also best avoided. Other social groups often feel discriminated against too in the use of language: people from minority ethnic or religious groups, homosexuals, the physically and mentally handicapped, and old people. In recent years the phenomenon of political correctness has taken these sensitivities to extremes that can seem excessive or even absurd; but you need to be aware of them in your writing.

Written and spoken English

The levels of formality in which English is used are called **registers**, which reflect the contexts in which they occur. English, like all languages, varies from the formal and technical at one extreme to the informal and casual at the other, depending on the type of communication involved: this can be conversation, informal writing, journalism, and broadcasting, or formal writing including essays, speeches, and more learned works. In everyday conversation, for example, we tend to use the personal pronouns *I* and *you* quite frequently, and resort to contractions such as *I've*, *you're*, and *don't* rather than the full forms *I have*, *you are*, and *do not*. Colloquial and slang words form a regular part of this type of usage. In more formal writing, colloquialisms are much less common, the indefinite pronoun *one* appears in place of the more conversational *you*, *upon* is likely to be used as well as *on*, and more formal words such as *ascertain* and *purchase* occur more often.

No one style of vocabulary and grammar is superior to another; it is their appropriateness to the occasion that matters.

Slang and informal language

Slang is the most informal level of language and is mainly restricted to casual conversation. It has no place in writing except at a familiar level (e.g. in personal letters) or when reporting conversation (e.g. in dialogue in a story).

Dr Johnson, whose famous *Dictionary of the English Language* was published in 1755, did not use the term *slang*; he used the disparaging term 'low words' instead, and the term *slang* comes into use a little later. But the existence of highly informal words, often associated with a particular class or occupation, is much older, and this type of vocabulary has been commented on for centuries, usually with disapproval.

In modern dictionaries the label *informal* is mostly used for vocabulary in general use that would once have been termed *slang*, while *slang* itself is restricted to the informal vocabulary associated with particular social groups, for example military slang, youth slang, and prison slang. Informal vocabulary typically falls into distinct kinds:

• extensions in meaning of established words and phrases (*to chill out* = to relax)
• shortenings of words (e.g. *aggro* from *aggression* and *cred* from *credibility*)
• compound and phrase-based formations (e.g. *badmouth*, *basket case*, and *must-have*)
• blends (e.g. *ginormous* from *gigantic* and *enormous*, *biopic* from *biographical* and *picture*)
• rhyming slang (e.g. *loaf* = loaf of bread = head)

- back slang, in which words are reversed (e.g. *yob* = boy).

Slang lies at the extreme end of informality. It contains a strong element of metaphor or verbal imagery, and has the potential to shock or offend. Its origins often lie in the language of particular occupations or social groups, such as racing, the criminal world, the armed forces, and youth (e.g. *ace*, *blatantly*, *cool*, and *wicked*). So the use of slang still has the social connotations of belonging to a group, and in English it has strong class associations. This helps to explain the widespread disapproval of using slang, since its use is associated with groups of people who are outside the circles that hold political power and are responsible for identifying standards. Informal and slang uses are especially prevalent in areas in which direct language is regarded as taboo or unsocial, such as death (e.g. *to peg out*, *to snuff it*), sexual activity (e.g. *to have it off*, *to screw*), and bodily functions (e.g. *to pee*, *to spend a penny*).

Slang is by its nature ephemeral, and relatively few words and uses pass into standard use. Exceptions include *bogus*, *clever*, *flog*, *joke*, *prim*, *rogue*, *sheer* (as in *sheer joy*), *snob*, and *tip* (meaning 'a gratuity'), which were all classed by Dr Johnson as 'low words'. By a reverse process, some words that were once in standard use have passed into slang (e.g. *arse*, *shit*, and *tit*).

We use informal language all the time in everyday conversation, but when we need to write our thoughts down in more formal language we can find it difficult to find the right expression in place of the one that is at the front of our minds. **Phrasal verbs**, i.e. a verb plus an adverb such as *bang on, cosy up, dumb down*, and *sex up*, form a major part of everyday informal vocabulary (although not all phrasal verbs are informal: *come back, go away, take over* are just a few examples of the many phrasal verbs that form a part of core English).

The table below provides some more formal alternatives to those phrasal verbs that can sometimes be too informal for use in writing. (You can also use the table in reverse!) For further material use a good thesaurus.

act up	misbehave, cause trouble; malfunction, go wrong
add up (as in *the situation doesn't add up*)	make sense, seem reasonable, ring true
ask around	make enquiries
back down	concede defeat, yield, give in
back off	withdraw
bawl out	reprimand, bawl, scold, admonish
beaver away	work hard, toil, labour
beef up	strengthen, build up, toughen
belt up	be quiet, quieten down, be silent, stop talking
boot out	dismiss, expel, get rid of
botch up	bungle, mishandle
be bowled over	overwhelmed, amazed, astounded, impressed
bring off	achieve, accomplish, succeed in
bunk off	play truant, be absent
cash in on	exploit, take advantage of
catch on	flourish, succeed, become popular, thrive

chat up	flirt with, make advances to
chew over	meditate on, mull over, think about, consider
chill out	relax
be choked up	be emotional
chuck in	give up, leave, resign from
clean out	bankrupt, impoverish, ruin
clear off	leave, go away, depart
clock up	achieve, register, record
cobble together	improvise, contrive, devise
come down on	rebuke, reprimand, admonish
come in for (e.g. criticism)	experience, sustain, incur
come out with	utter, express, exclaim
come up (as in *something's come up*)	arise, occur, present itself
come up with	suggest, propose, devise, put forward
conk out	malfunction, stop working
cook up	devise, concoct, invent
cop out	avoid, shirk, dodge, skip
cosy up to	cultivate, curry favour with, befriend, ingratiate oneself with
cotton on to	understand, come to realize
cough up	provide, pay
crack on	persevere
crop up	occur, appear
cry off	withdraw
be cut up	be upset, be distressed
dish out	serve, provide with
do away with	abolish, eliminate, discard, remove, get rid of

drag on	persist, continue, be protracted
drag out	prolong, protract, extend, lengthen
drop by/in/round	call, visit
eye up	ogle, stare at, leer at
face up to (a situation)	accept, confront, acknowledge, admit
fall off (as in *admissions have fallen off*)	decline, decrease, diminish, go down
fall through	fail, collapse, be unsuccessful, come to nothing
figure out	fathom, calculate, reckon, work out
firm up	finalize, confirm, make definite
fish out	extract, remove, retrieve, extricate
fix up	organize, arrange, plan
fizzle out	peter out, die off, wane, come to nothing
fob off (as in *fob someone off with something*)	saddle, deceive, lumber, burden, put off
fob off (as in *fob something off on someone*)	impose, unload
fold up	fail, collapse, be unsuccessful, come to nothing
freak out	go crazy, lose control, panic, crack
get along	be friendly, be compatible
get away with	escape blame for, escape punishment for

get by	manage, cope, survive, subsist
get in on	become involved in, contribute to
get off	be acquitted, escape punishment
get out of	escape, avoid, evade, shirk
go back on (e.g. a promise)	renege on, break, fail to honour, retract
go in for	practise, take part in, enjoy, relish
go under	fail, collapse, be unsuccessful, become bankrupt
hang about	loiter, linger, delay, procrastinate
be hung up on	be anxious about, be obsessed with
head off (as in *head off an argument*)	forestall, avoid, avert, prevent
head off (as in *head someone off*)	intercept, divert, deflect
hold out (as in *hold out against an attack*)	resist, withstand
hold out (as in *supplies holding out*)	last, continue
hype up	publicize, advertise, promote
iron out (problems)	resolve, rectify, settle, clear up, straighten out
jog along	make progress, manage, cope
jolly along	encourage, urge
keep on at	harass, badger, pester, chivvy, nag

kick in	start working, start up
kick off	start, begin, get under way
knock back	consume, drink, get through
knock off	stop work
knock up	improvise, devise, concoct
knuckle down	start work
lay on	provide, supply
be laid up	be indisposed
let on	admit, confess to
let up	abate, lessen; relax
look down on	disapprove of, disparage
look out	beware, be vigilant, be on one's guard
look over	peruse, review, read through, check, monitor
be looking up	improve, be encouraging
lump together	amalgamate
make off with	appropriate, steal
make out	manage, cope, survive
make up	be reconciled
make up to	ingratiate oneself with
measure up	be adequate
mess about/around with	interfere with, meddle with, tinker with
mess up	bungle, spoil, botch
mess with	become involved with
miss out	exclude, leave out
be mixed up with	be involved with
muck about/around with	interfere with, meddle with, tinker with
muck in	contribute, participate
muck up	bungle, spoil, botch

muddle through	manage, cope, survive
nod off	fall asleep, doze off
opt out	withdraw, refuse, decline to take part in
own up	confess, admit a wrong
pack in	finish, give up, renounce, resign from
pack up	stop working, fail
pan out	develop, proceed
pass up	forgo, go without, decline
patch up	repair
perk up	revive, recover
pick up	improve, revive
pick up on	react to
play up	behave badly, work badly
plug away	work hard
polish off	complete, finish; devour, consume
pop in	call, visit
pop up	appear, occur, materialize
psych oneself up	steel oneself, nerve oneself, prepare oneself, brace oneself
pull out	withdraw, retire, leave, resign
pull through	recover, improve, rally, get better
pull up	stop, come to a stop, draw up
push off	leave, withdraw
put off	deter, discourage, demotivate; postpone
put out	issue, publish, broadcast
put up with	tolerate, accept, suffer
rattle off	recite, reel off, list

rein in	control, restrain, curb, check, constrain
rip off	swindle, cheat, overcharge
roll up	arrive, assemble, gather
round off	complete, finish
rule out	exclude, reject, dismiss, eliminate
run in	arrest, apprehend
run up	incur, accumulate
screw up	bungle, spoil, botch
set up	establish, institute
show up	arrive, appear; be visible, be conspicuous, be obvious
show up	shame, embarrass, humiliate, mortify
shut up	stop talking, be quiet
size up	assess, evaluate, appraise, estimate
sniff out	discover, detect
be snowed under	be inundated
soak up	absorb
sound out	investigate
spell out	explain, elaborate on
split up	separate
stand down	withdraw, resign
step down	withdraw, resign
step up	increase, intensify
stick up for	support, defend
stir up	engender, aggravate, cause
stop by/off	visit
string along	deceive
stump up	provide money, pay

sum up	summarize
tail off	decrease
take away	remove, withdraw
take in	deceive, fool, cheat
take off	succeed, flourish; do impression of
take on	employ, recruit
take on	challenge, compete with
take over	assume control, dominate
take up	assume, continue with
talk down to	patronize, be condescending towards
tear down	demolish, destroy
tell off	reprimand, scold
throw off	dispel, dismiss, get rid of
throw up	engender, cause, bring about
tie up	fasten, secure
tip off	warn, advise
top up	replenish, refill, refresh
touch off	provoke, instigate, cause
trigger off	provoke, instigate, cause
turn off	deter, discourage, demotivate
turn out (as in *see how things turn out*)	develop, happen, occur, come about
turn up	arrive, assemble, gather
water down	dilute, weaken
weigh down	oppress, burden
weigh up	assess, evaluate
whip up	provoke, stimulate
wind down	decline, reduce
wind up	close, discontinue; provoke, irritate

wipe out	remove, erase, delete
work up	produce, stimulate
write off	dismiss, disregard, reject, ignore

A dress-code for language: formality and over-formality

Different modes of writing and speaking call for different kinds of language, just as styles of dress are appropriate to different social occasions. At one extreme there is the language of legal documents, business, and academic monographs; at the other there is the language of everyday conversation, with a broad range between. The language of broadcasting and journalism, for example, has become much less formal in recent years, to the disapproval of many who see the media as having a role in maintaining language norms.

Choice of vocabulary differs according to register. At the most formal end, a machine might be said to be *malfunctioning*; in everyday language it will be described as *not working*, and at the informal extreme it will be said to be *bust* or *acting up* or *knackered*. Formal words occur in instructions and notices: *alight* (from a bus or train), *conveyance* (instead of *vehicle*), *enquire* (instead of *ask*), *notify* (instead of *tell*), and *select* (instead of *choose*). In more general contexts, *purchase* is more formal than *buy*, *edifice* than *building*, *endeavour* than *try*, *evince* than *show*, and *purloin* than *steal*.

Remember that a formal word can be as inappropriate in general contexts as an informal one. Some formal words occur only in official documents, such as contracts, and should not be adopted into general use, where their effect can be stilted, pretentious, or even ridiculous.

But sometimes they can afford humour. If you scan through the words in a dictionary (many of the words in the table on pp. 192–5, for example), you will find them marked as 'formal or humorous', because although their primary use is technical and formal, they also have the power to amuse. Ask someone if they care to *imbibe*, for example, and you will raise a smile.

Effects such as these are sometimes useful in writing, but you need to use them sparingly.

Too many abstract nouns: abstractitis

Abstractitis was a term invented by Sir Ernest Gowers, a senior Whitehall civil servant who wrote a famous guide to usage called *The Complete Plain Words*. He was warning against excessive use of abstract nouns, especially those based on verbs, such as *actualization, desirability, initiation*, and *mutuality*, which are cumbersome and obscure the meaning. In these cases, verbs – sometimes just the verbs that lie behind the overblown abstract nouns – are usually better and clearer:

? *They protested against the undesirability of this course of action.*

✓ *They protested that this course of action was undesirable.*

? *The initiation of the proposal was imminent.*

✓ *The proposal was about to be put into effect.*

Some formal and official-sounding words and phrases and their equivalents

abjure	renounce
abnegate	renounce
accede to	grant, allow
accordingly	so
abrogate	repeal a law
acquaint oneself with	find out about
adjure	urge
alight	get off (a train or bus)
alleviate	ease, lessen, reduce
anterior to	prior to
apparel	clothing
appellation	name
appurtenant	belonging
as a consequence of	because of, as a result of
ascertain	find out
behove	be a duty (for someone)
cession	giving up of a right
cogitate	think about something
cognizance	knowledge *or* awareness
comestible	item of food
commensurate with	in proportion to, consistent with
commodious	spacious and comfortable
compendious	thorough but concise
comport oneself	behave (in a certain way)
concomitant	typically associated
confute	prove wrong
conjoin	combine
conveyance	vehicle
corroboration	proof, support
delectation	pleasure

denizen	inhabitant
denominate	name
denomination	name
discontinue	stop, end
dispatch	send
domicile	place of residence
edifice	building
efficacious	effective
emanate from	come from, stem from
emolument	salary *or* fee
erroneous	wrong, mistaken
essay	attempt
exiguous	very small
facilitate	assist, help
foregather	come together
gainsay	deny *or* contradict
gratuity	tip
habitation	home
henceforth	from now (*or* then) on
hirsute	hairy
hitherto	until now (*or* then)
imbibe	drink alcohol
implement	carry out, put into practice
imprecation	curse
in accordance with	in line with, following
incommode	inconvenience
initiate	start, begin, put into practice
in the interim	meanwhile
lachrymose	tearful
laud	praise
malfunction	fail to work
manifold	many and various

necessitate	require, need, call for
opine	state as one's opinion
oration	formal speech
parturition	childbirth
pecuniary	to do with money, financial
penurious	having no money, destitute
perambulate	walk about
perambulator	pram
perquisite	special privilege
pertinacious	stubborn
peruse	read carefully
plenitude	abundance
postprandial	after a meal
predecease	die before someone
preprandial	before a meal
prestidigitation	conjuring tricks
purchase	buy
purloin	steal
pursuance	the carrying out of an activity
pursuant to	in accordance with
rebarbative	repellent
rectitude	correct behaviour
refractory	stubborn and difficult
regardful of	having in mind
repast	meal
sanctitude	holiness
spirituous	containing alcohol
subjoin	add at the end
subscribe	sign a document
subscription	signature
tonsorial	to do with hairdressing
torpefy	make numb

turpitude	wickedness
utilize	use
veracious	speaking the truth
verify	check, prove
voracious	eagerly eating

Making it hard to read: jargon and gobbledegook

All professions and special spheres of activity develop a special vocabulary that its participants use to communicate effectively with one another; medicine, law, gastronomy, sociology, and (most recently) computing are well-known examples. This special vocabulary is called **jargon**. Other domains, notably journalism, use special words and idioms that are not normally found in general use: *probe* for *investigation* or *investigate*, *quiz* for *interrogate*, *package* for *deal*, and *swap* for *transplant* (in the medical sense). These are typically short words that make for concise expression in newspaper headlines (*Shooting suspect escape drama*). Another common stylistic feature of newspaper reports – also adopted in the interests of brevity – is to treat people's occupations and physical characteristics as if they were military titles; for example:

We spoke to computer software company director Paul Smith from Solihull.
One victim of the outbreak was mother-of-two Diane Westbrook.
Blonde actress Jennifer Elliot rubbed shoulders with the stars of Hollywood.

This style is inelegant and should not be adopted in ordinary writing.

In some contexts, especially where legal definitions and obligations are involved, the need for precision requires the use of special terminology because it has to stand up to constant scrutiny. This famous Department of Health definition of *container* won a Golden Bull award from the Plain English Campaign in 2004:

'Container', in relation to an investigational medicinal product, means the bottle, jar, box, packet or other receptacle which contains or is to contain it, not being a capsule, cachet or other article in which the product is or is to be administered, and where any such receptacle is or is to be contained in another such receptacle, includes the former but does not include the latter receptacle.

But criticism here is misplaced. This is not a general description, but a detailed definition necessary for people working in the medical profession who need to know exactly what counts as a container and what doesn't (it isn't as straightforward as you might think), and it needs to dot every *i* and cross every *t* to avoid misunderstandings and loopholes.

Problems arise when members of the professions need to communicate with the public at large; then, jargon can easily become gobbledegook. Another – and much more justified – award went to British Telecom for this email to a member of the public who was enquiring about provision of cable networks:

BT have started processing the first stage of our MPF orders, i.e. the line test and production of a line characteristics report. However with the second stage (i.e. physically installing the metallic facility path between the customers line and the Trilogy equipment) they will only walk one or two orders through the system Thursday of next week.

What the recipient needed to know was that the line had been tested and a report written, but that the next stage of work, the actual laying of the cable (which is what the 'metallic facility path' is) would be subject to delay because there was a limit on the orders that could be processed on the following Thursday. At least, this appears to be the meaning. It could have been expressed much more clearly, instead of spewing technical jargon into a message intended to give some basic information to a non-specialist user.

Plain English, i.e. ordinary English that everyone can understand, requires clarity as well as accuracy. It is unlikely that you will be tempted to write in the style of the BT memo, which represents an extreme. But there are dangers whenever you are writing for a general audience about specialist areas of knowledge or information. In these circumstances it is important to avoid convoluted, obfuscating language typified by the use of words such as *aforesaid, in the event of, thereto, pursuant to,* and *incumbent on,* and others listed in the table above, as well as technical jargon that will confuse anyone who is not specially trained.

Two special kinds of formal words come in the categories called genteelisms and archaisms. These can form effective uses of language, but they usually sound affected and self-conscious.

Being over-polite: genteelisms

A genteelism is a less familiar and seemingly more polite word borrowed from formal or technical usage and substituted for a word that is considered distasteful, improper, or simply vulgar. Genteelisms are therefore euphemisms taken a stage further, because they are forced into an inappropriate register. Judgements about this type of vocabulary change from one generation to the next, and some that were regarded with scorn in the past no longer seem to offend. A few remaining examples include *desire* for *want*, *endeavour* for *try*, *hard of hearing* for *deaf*, *enquire* for *ask*, *peruse* for *read*, *perspire* for *sweat*, and phrases such as *retire for the night* for *go to bed*.

Being old-fashioned: archaisms

There are certain words and phrases that no longer form a part of everyday language but are still used for special effect, especially in literature: these are called **archaisms**. Some archaisms still have a role to play in modern English, while others are real period pieces that are normally used mainly for humorous effect. Examples of the second kind are *peradventure* and *whilom* but there is still a use for *betimes*, *erstwhile*, *goodly*, *lest*, *nay*, *perchance*, and *unbeknown*:

*Had she some power **unbeknown** to herself, which smoothed her way through life?*
*She wondered how his **erstwhile** mentors would react once they learned what he had become.*

*Do you think, **perchance**, that this is the right time to reveal our identity?*

Lest is a formal word, but it is relatively common and is one of the great mainstays of the English subjunctive (note *catch* in the following example):

*He dared venture out only on the balmiest of days, **lest he catch** cold.* (The alternative, *in case he caught cold*, is more typical of everyday language but much less elegant.)

The centuries-old prefix *a-* (as in *birds aflutter* and *out a-hunting*) is still used to good effect, especially to give an archaic flavour in contexts rooted in the past:

Spectators would fall a-talking of the fashionableness of bicycling.

Archaisms in literature

> *Dear father, prithee add thyself to that venerable company ere the soup cools.*
>
> Charles Reade, *The Cloister and the Hearth*, 1861

> *If Mimi's cup runneth over, it runneth over with decency rather than with anything more vital.*
>
> Anita Brookner, *Family and Friends*, 1985 (alluding to Psalms 23:5)

> *The whole creation groaneth and travaileth in pain together.*
>
> Iris Murdoch, *The Book and the Brotherhood*, 1987 (alluding to Romans 8:22)

Overdoing it: hackneyed words and clichés

A **hackneyed** word or phrase is one that has become practically meaningless from overuse, such as *nice* or *fascinating*. The word *hackneyed* comes from the district of London called Hackney. In the days when it was a village in the country it was famous for breeding horses suitable for pulling carriages. These became known as *hackney carriages* (which is still the official name for London taxis), and the horses, which were often overworked and suffered from exhaustion, were called *hacks*. So a hackneyed word or expression is a piece of language that has been treated rather like an old worn-out horse: not much use to anyone.

You will probably have your own mental (or actual) list of words that irritate you from overuse. In their right place they are useful, but too often they are used without any reference to real meaning. Below is a list you might like to compare it with. There may be words in it that are less bothersome to you but are known to cause problems so that you should be aware of them. Note that there is no grammatical objection to any of these words, at least not in normal usage; the objection is based entirely on overuse. Some hackneyed words are technical terms that are precise in their original meaning but have been adopted in over-generalized contexts without a real basis of meaning, e.g. *interface* and *parameter*.

actually (redundant use as in *actually I don't want any more*)

basically (redundant use as in *there is basically nothing wrong*)

definitely (redundant use as in
 it's definitely time to go)
dichotomy (= distinction)
dimension (= aspect or factor)
escalate (= increase)
fascinating
infrastructure
interface
lifestyle
meaningful

nice
obscene (= repellent)
parameter
persona (= a person's character)
pivotal
scenario (= situation)
simplistic (= oversimplified)
utilize (= use)
viability

A hackneyed phrase is also called a **cliché**, a French word having the same meaning as in English and originally a term for a photographic negative or printing plate, which produces a cast for printing called a *stereotype* (another word that has spawned a language term). Eric Partridge, the New Zealand-born lexicographer of slang, compiled a *Dictionary of Clichés* in 1940, pointing to such phrases as *add insult to injury*, *a fate worse than death*, and *to nip in the bud* as examples to be wary of. When he came to revise his work in the 1970s, he declared that 'the situation seems to have become worse', and in recent years we have seen the addition of such interview gap-fillers as *at this moment in time*, *at the end of the day*, *the bottom line is* (from the language of corporate accountants), and *taking everything into consideration* (a favourite with civil servants). Partridge asked whether clichés are not sometimes justifiable, and answered 'To say "Never" would be going too far.' They are sentence-fillers and sentence-fillers can be useful, especially in speech, when there is less time to invent alternatives. But in writing they can give an impression of laziness or at least an absence of imagination. Below are some of the more notorious clichés to avoid:

to add insult to injury
all things considered
approximately (= about)
as a matter of fact
at daggers drawn
at the end of the day
at this moment in time
the bottom line (is)
by leaps and bounds
by no means certain
by the skin of one's teeth
a crisis situation
a different ball game
the end of the road
to enter a minefield
to explore every avenue
fair and square
to fall on deaf ears
far and wide
a fatal flaw
a fate worse than death
few and far between
from the bottom of one's heart
a grievous error
to grind to a halt
here today and gone tomorrow
highly improbable
in the dim and distant past
in the event that (= if)

in the neighbourhood of
   (= about, roughly)
in this day and age
to keep a low profile
a kindred spirit
to know the ropes
last but not least
to lead a dog's life
to leave no stone unturned
a level playing field
the long and the short of it
the mind boggles
the name of the game
to nip in the bud
on the back burner
the picture of health
a quantum leap
rotten at the core
six of one and half a dozen of
   the other
to step into the breach
to take it as read
to take on board
taking everything into
   consideration
the thin end of the wedge
until such time as
to welcome with open arms

He was, however, on the whole, taking all things into consideration, by and large, not to put too fine a point on it, reasonably well self-sufficient.

Anthony Burgess, *Mr Enderby*, 1963

Offensive language

Language is notoriously capable of upsetting and offending people. Sometimes this is deliberate, from the choice of ideas and the words to represent them, and the issue is then social or political rather than linguistic. To use any of the well-known 'four-letter' words in an abusive way is to resort to the most offensive English words that have general reference. The type of words that fulfil this role change from one age to another: in the past they have been words about death and money, and in our own day they are words about sex and bodily functions.

There are other words that are in themselves derogatory to the point of being offensive (usually informal words such as *prat* and *nerd*). There are also words and uses that can cause unintentional offence. You may not be aware that there is a danger of causing offence at all, or you may not be aware how offensive a particular expression can be. Because a word is entered in a dictionary does not mean it is safe to use it. Dictionaries exist to give information about all kinds of words, and they are usually careful to warn users, usually by some kind of label such as *offensive*, that a particular word is derogatory or offensive.

Stereotypes

Stereotypes are like clichés but arise from general notions and descriptions as much as from particular words. Those based on race, ethnic origin, religion, gender, and other characteristics are among the commonest types of offensiveness in language. They are very old in English, occurring frequently in the works of Shakespeare and his contemporaries, for example. (You don't have to look very far in *The Merchant of Venice* or *Othello* to find them.) Usually they have more to do with popular prejudices and associations about people than with historical truth. Idioms such as *street Arab* and *young Turk* are no longer acceptable and you should avoid them; in fact they are falling out of use. Calling a woman a *bitch* or a *cow* is much more offensive than calling a man a *dog* or a *weasel* (uses that now have little effect and therefore sound quaint and dated), and calling an ineffectual man an *old woman*, though less obviously offensive than some uses, is more likely to upset people today than formerly.

Names for peoples

Greater care than ever is needed in using slang or informal names for peoples. Some words can be relatively innocuous or even affectionate (e.g. *Brit* = 'a British person', *Yank* = 'an American') and the tone of voice can do much to mitigate the bad effect, as well as the context in which the word is used, and your relationship with the person or people you are speaking to or writing for. Some ethnic terms of this kind are, however, much stronger in effect and will always cause offence (*dago* for 'Spaniard', *Jap* for 'Japanese', and *Yid* for 'Jew').

The origins of some of these words show them to be almost absurdly trivial and childish (e.g. *Frog* = 'Frenchman', because people famously eat frogs' legs in France, and *Kraut* = 'a person from Germany', where sauerkraut is eaten). Others are fanciful formations: for example the Australian word *Pommy* for 'an English immigrant' is derived from *pomegranate* and forms a play on the word *immigrant*. Others give rise to bogus accounts of their origins (so-called folk etymologies): for example, *wog* meaning 'foreigner' is supposedly an acronym of *westernized* (or *wily*) *oriental gentleman*, although the more likely explanation is that it is a shortening of *golliwog*.

Offensive words tend to have a limited life cycle and many have declined in use and sound dated. *Nigger* was always a highly offensive term for a black-skinned person, and was meant to be. Now *Negro* (and the feminine form *Negress*) are also regarded as offensive both in Britain and in America, and since the 1960s the term *black* (with a small initial letter) has replaced them. In Britain, the term *Paki* for a person from Pakistan or the Indian subcontinent generally is one of the most offensive ethnic terms in use.

Words based on disability
Another kind of use that causes great offence is that based on people's physical or mental disabilities. Calling someone *spastic* to mean 'stupid or incompetent', or using *cretin* to mean 'a stupid person', insults groups of people who suffer from the actual disabilities denoted

by the primary meanings of these words. So serious is the insult that the words cannot be used any more in their first meanings, because the offensive overtones have rubbed off on them. This means that we have to use alternative words, e.g. *person with cerebral palsy* instead of *spastic* and *person with Down's syndrome* instead of *mongol*, and *disabled person* instead of *cripple* (which has developed an extended meaning, as in *an industry crippled by strikes*, that is not in itself offensive).

Sexism and gender issues

Radical changes in the role of women and attitudes about them have meant that language has had to change too, although it tends to change more slowly than society as a whole does. For centuries, English has made distinctions between men and women that are now regarded as unnecessary and patronizing, or even offensive. While the language is catching up with public opinion, there are bound to be difficult areas. Although English does not contain as much grammatical gender as some other languages, we still have male and female pronouns (*he, she, her, him, his*), words for men and women (*man* and *woman*, *boy* and *girl*, *bachelor* and *spinster*, and so on), and feminine forms of certain words, notably occupations and in names of animals (such as *actress*, *manageress*, and *lioness*).

In spite of the reduced role of grammatical gender in English, there are still problem areas to watch out for:

• when using pronouns referring to people regardless

of their sex (the *he or she* problem). Traditionally, masculine forms have been used, but this is no longer acceptable: you will find guidance on this issue in section 1. Artificial devices, such as the invented words *s/he*, *hesh*, and *wself*, have not caught on because they are impossible to use in speech and look awkward in print.

• when there is a feminine form of a word for a role or occupation, which has survived by convention rather than because of a real need (mainly words ending in *-ess* and *-woman*, e.g. *actress*, *manageress*; but some are still needed, e.g. titles such as *baroness*, *empress*, *duchess*, and terms in which the distinction matters, e.g. *goddess, governess*). There is more on this under **Terms for occupations**, p. 209.

• when pairs of words for men and women have different associations (for example, *bachelor* has romantic overtones whereas *spinster* sounds negative and uninteresting; *gentleman* is a term of respect whereas *lady* can sound affected or condescending; *master* always denotes authority whereas *mistress* has a meaning that implies submission).

• when positive-sounding words based on masculine roots have no feminine or neutral counterpart (such as *masterly* and *masterpiece*), and deprecatory words based on feminine roots either have no masculine or neutral counterpart (such as *charwoman*, *hag*, and *old maid*) or have one that is much more positive (such as *mistress* contrasted with *lover*).

• when neutral words are masculine in form but need to be applied to both sexes (such as *mankind* and *man-made*).

• when referring to men and women in different ways (e.g. calling a male person a *man* and a female person a *girl*).

Some of the more specific words are falling out of use. We now talk about *cleaners* and not *charwomen*, and we would say that someone was *unmarried* rather than calling them a *bachelor* or *spinster*. Useful neutral occupational terms have come into use, including *firefighter* in place of *fireman*, *flight attendant* and *cabin crew* in place of *air hostess(es)*, *headteacher* in place of *headmaster* and *headmistress*, and *police officer* in place of *policeman* and *policewoman*. *Humankind* is gradually taking over from *mankind*.

There are other ways to be careful about handling gender in language:

• by taking care to match the tone and style of masculine and feminine references:

? *The meeting elected a further eight members, four ladies and four men.*

✓ *The meeting elected a further eight members, four women and four men.*

• by avoiding words that are strongly masculine in form when they are meant to have a general reference:

? *The caves are man-made, hewn out of the rock by hand.*

✓ *The caves are not natural, but hewn out of the rock by hand.*

• by avoiding those feminine words for roles and occupations that cause offence. This is discussed more fully in the next few paragraphs.

Terms for occupations
words ending in -ess *and* -ette

The words used to name people and describe what they do are very important to them. Traditionally, terms for occupations have had masculine and feminine forms, such as *actor* and *actress*, *manager* and *manageress*, and *usher* and *usherette*. Words ending in *-ess* for feminine roles and occupations are very old in English, with early forms recorded from the 14th century or even earlier (e.g. *countess*, *duchess*, *mistress*).

The fact that these words are formed by adapting a masculine word by means of a special feminine suffix suggests that the male form is the standard one and the female forms are a kind of afterthought or deviation, although this is less true of pairs such as *chairman* and *chairwoman*, which convey a greater sense of equivalence. Today, there is less need to identify men and women routinely in this way unless the distinction still matters, as it does with titles such as *baroness* and *duchess*, forms where the male equivalent has a different meaning, such as *governess*, and terms in which the feminine status is significant, as with *goddess* and animal names such as *lioness*.

Remember that some titles (e.g. *ambassadress* and *mayoress*) refer to the wife of an official, whereas a woman who holds the office in her own right would be named with the *-or* forms (*ambassador*, *mayor*). Other *-ess* forms remain acceptable in specific contexts (e.g. *manageress* when referring to a restaurant or hotel) but not all.

The racial words *Jewess* and *Negress* cause great offence and should be avoided except when referring historically to the past.

Feminine words ending in -*ette* (e.g. *usherette*) and -*enne* (e.g. *comedienne*) are usually seen as the most patronizing of all these forms and they are rapidly disappearing.

-man, -woman, *and* -person

Take care to use words ending in -*man*, such as *chairman* and *craftsman*, only when you are referring to a man. Some words in -*man* are still common because the relevant occupation is still mostly done by men. For example, *postal worker* is the neutral term for people working for the Royal Mail, but *postman* is still widely used to refer to the person who delivers post because nearly all the people who do this are men.

In the 1970s, a gender-neutral suffix, -*person*, came into use in place of -*man* to denote occupations: the first words formed this way were *chairperson* and *spokesperson*. Since then it has spread slowly to other words (e.g. *barperson* and *salesperson*), but they can be awkward and even comic in use and forms ending in -*woman* are still often preferred (e.g. *spokeswoman*).

It is also best to avoid expressions such as *woman* (or *lady*) *doctor*, which imply that a male is normal in this role, unless there are special reasons for specifying the gender. The same now goes, in reverse, for *male nurse*.

Political correctness

Sensitivities about language have been greatly increased, and raised from the level of language to that of communication more generally, by the movement called political correctness (or PC), which arose in America in the 1980s and rapidly spread to Britain and other parts of the world. PC goes much further than the kinds of uses we have been looking at so far by vilifying language that might cause offence in much less direct ways. A prime target has been metaphor and figurative uses of words such as *the black economy* and *being deaf to something* (= unwilling to listen to it), and other words thought to be offensive to various groups because of the coincidence of words and meanings rather than any deliberate intention to offend.

Attitudes to gender issues are a good deal more intense as well, with words such as *manhandle* and *manhole* equally rejected. At its extremes it can be linguistically ridiculous, e.g. dismissing words such as *history* because of the coincidence of form in its first syllable with the masculine possessive pronoun *his*. The difficulty with words of this kind is that no satisfactory equivalent words are available: *personhandle* and *personhole* sound absurd, and *herstory* (though sometimes heard) is no more than a sterile contrivance.

This philosophy also tries to find alternative words that give a more positive aspect to negative or undesirable qualities, replacing *failure* with *achievement deficiency*, *disabled* with *differently abled*, and *unemployed* with *non-waged*. Disabilities and other human difficulties are expressed with the more positive-sounding word *challenged*: *backward* and *educationally subnormal* become *intellectually challenged*, *short* becomes *vertically challenged*, and *disabled* becomes *physically challenged*.

In language terms a movement such as this is doomed to eventual failure. Even if the world were to adopt its principles overnight, the language would soon catch up on itself. Words pick up their flavour from the meaning and use they are put to, and in time all the words now proposed as neutral alternatives would be sure to go the way of the words they are replacing: in fact *challenged* is already being noted as a term of general abuse.

Political correctness therefore represents an extreme. It is important to apply common sense to all uses of words, and to strike a balance between avoiding language sensitivities and communicating effectively with people without distracting them with self-conscious evasions or patronizing them with artificial or anodyne inventions.

5
Problems hitlist

In the first two sections we looked at the elements and patterns of English grammar and usage and identified the main systematic difficulties that repeatedly arise from these patterns and cause people uncertainty: dangling participles, split infinitives, where prepositions go, and so on. In this section you will find an alphabetical listing of words and phrases that give rise to particular problems to do with their meanings or the ways in which they relate to other words in writing sentences.

according as *or* to?

*The giant panda faces a new threat – global warming – **according to** a report published today.*
*People should pay **according to** the value of their property.*

The more common form is *according to*, which is called a complex preposition because it serves as a preposition (like *by* or *with*), as in the two sentences given above. In the first sentence, *according to* means 'on the authority of' and in the second it means 'in accordance with' or 'in proportion to'. These are its two main meanings.

Less common is the combination *according as*, which is a conjunction and is followed by a clause containing a verb:

*The myth that a man makes has transformations **according as** he sees himself as hero or villain.*
*How the committee is proceeding is made more or less difficult **according as** the chairman is less or more efficient.*

This construction used to be frowned on (e.g. by H W Fowler in *Modern English Usage*), but it has become well established and is now unexceptionable. Occasionally one finds the extended construction *according as to*, but this can become awkward and preferable alternatives are often available, e.g. *depending on*:

? *Actions are right or wrong **according as to** [✓ depending on] whether they increase or decrease the amount of happiness in the world.*

aggravate

It is better to keep *aggravate* in reserve for its primary and more useful meaning 'to make more serious':

✓ *The council is now proposing to **aggravate** the situation even more by having a park and ride in the peat bog.*

Its meaning 'to annoy' (which is admittedly more common, and by no means merely recent: see below) will find disfavour in many quarters, harmless though it is in ordinary conversation:

? *Putting a bus lane in is only going to **aggravate** [✓ annoy or irritate] people.*

Therefore, Florence, pray let us see that you have some strength of mind, and do not selfishly aggravate the distress in which your poor papa is plunged.

Charles Dickens, *Dombey and Son*, 1848

She only wanted to threaten him and aggravate him, for speaking to her as he had just spoken.

Wilkie Collins, *The Woman in White*, 1860

agree with *or* to?

It is important to remember the difference between agreeing *with* (= having the same opinion as) someone or something and agreeing *to* (= consenting to) something.

*He was always stimulating, even though I did not always **agree with** his ideas.*
*Most teachers would **agree with** this statement.*
*He **agreed with** Wordsworth that the greens of summer were monotonous.*

*I immediately **agreed to** the UK being responsible for the investigation.*
*Iraq **agreed to** a meeting of military leaders to discuss ceasefire arrangements.*

You cannot *agree to* someone, but you can *agree to* someone (or someone's) doing something:

*We will **agree to** your joining the team on certain conditions.*

The verb *agree* is also transitive (i.e. takes an object) with the meaning 'come to an agreement about' as in *agreeing terms*, and it can take a *that*-clause (corresponding to *agree with*) and a *to*-infinitive (corresponding to *consent*):

*I **agree that** some people find it difficult to find all the money at once.*
*It has already been **agreed to** reduce the conference to one day.*

aim at *or* to?

*We asked the women to **aim at** eating three meals each day.*
*The series **aimed to** introduce English readers to literary theory.*

In its figurative or abstract senses, i.e. outside the realm of real-life blows and shooting, the verb *aim* can be followed either by *at* with an *-ing* verb (as in the first sentence above) or by a *to*-infinitive (as in the second). The *at* construction is rather more vivid and tends to conjure up a stronger image (and some language purists prefer it as being closer to the usage in physical senses) while the *to* construction follows the analogy of more abstract verbs such as *intend* and *seek* (which can often be used instead, sometimes to better effect):

*The artificial intelligence community **aim at** producing computer programs that can 'understand' the input.*
*Eliot's play **aimed to** penetrate beyond the 'frightful' to a deeper sense of universal evil.*
*He **aimed to** operate an air route towards the end of this year.*

ain't

Perhaps it hardly needs saying that this negative form of the verb *be*, used to mean *am not, is not,* and *are not*, should be avoided like the plague, as in the judgement of many it is one of the most forceful signs of illiteracy that the language can offer. Exceptions apply when quoting, when reproducing dialogue, and in similar cases.

albeit

This is a useful word that conveniently combines elements of the meaning contained in *if*, *though*, and *admittedly*. It is a pity to regard *albeit* as a quaint archaism, because although it sounds like one it has a useful role to play as an economical link word with rather more punch than *if*, *while*, and other alternatives:

*Wesker was struck by another (**albeit** minor) disaster.*
*The Princess of Wales continued to shop at Laura Ashley, **albeit** with a bodyguard.*
*This approach tries to produce a match between child and task, **albeit** recognizing that modifications will have to be made.*

It is less often used as a conjunction, followed by a *that*-clause (or a clause with *that* omitted), but here the alternative *even though* can be more straightforward and just as effective. *Albeit that* is found most often in legal and other official contexts:

*The conversion of one kind of cocaine to another was production of a substance 'by other means' **albeit that** the same generic term, cocaine, covered both substances.*

all right / alright

The form still generally preferred is *all right*, written in full as two words. The contracted form *alright* is widely disliked despite the analogy of *almighty* and *altogether* (see below), although it is more acceptable as an adverb (as in the fourth example below):

*'I hope your husband is **all right**,' Mr Hobbs said.*
*My knee feels **all right** when I'm running.*
*Oh, I'm desperate **all right**.*

? *Alright, shut the door and come in.*
✗ *These reports are **alright** [✓ all right] as far as they go.*
✗ *As soon as she spoke to Diane she knew she'd be **alright** [✓ all right].*

altogether / all together

It is important to remember that *altogether* and *all together* have different meanings. *Altogether* is an adverb meaning 'in every way, entirely' (as in *this idea is not altogether new*). *All together* means 'everyone or everything together' (as in *it has been good to be all together as a squad*).

There are other cases where *all* and *together* need to keep their separate identity:

*The moral outrage generated over gambling threatens to open up a political Pandora's box of values which will chip away at the cement **binding us all together**. (Together here goes with bind.)*

among / amongst

In British English, *among* and *amongst* are largely inter-changeable, although *among* is much more common (about five times more, according to the British National Corpus, a language database of 100 million words). They can both refer to concrete senses (refer-ring to physical position) and abstract senses (referring to notional place in a group):

*Foxgloves seem to self-seed in the shade **among** the tobacco plants.*
*Talk was intense **among** the youngsters.*
*Judges are required to be selected from **amongst** practising barristers.*

Both words are used with plural nouns, and are also common with collective nouns that imply 'more than one', this category being broad in scope:

*They are to be found everywhere, even **among** the old, the disabled, the celibate, the deserted, and the bereaved.*
*They had been picking bilberries, stooping over the little tough bushes **among** the heather.*
*I strolled **among** the boxwood as if I was the keenest of gardeners.*

If the noun is markedly singular, it is usually better to use *amid* or *amidst* or *in the midst of*:

? Amongst [✓ *amidst* or *in the midst of*] all the noise of London Bridge Station, I slept like the proverbial top.

and *in* **come and see / go and look / try and do it**

Come and see what we've found.
*One of our specialist nurses will arrange to **come and** see you.*
*I will **go and** look at the tree and see if we can climb up to the apples.*
*Let's **try and** get on this boat.*

This idiomatic use of *and* in place of *to* is shared by the three verbs *come*, *go*, and *try*. It is most common in the present and future tenses, and especially in the imperative (giving an instruction, as in the first example above). In the second example, *and* usefully avoids an awkward repetition of *to*.

Come and *go* (but not *try*) can also be followed by *and* in the past:

*He phoned her that night, then **went and saw** her.*
*I tried to [**✗** and] **open it**.*

These uses are typical in everyday conversation, but less suitable in more formal and official writing, where a *to*-infinitive is generally preferable.

anticipate

There is a lot of misunderstanding about this word. Properly and usefully used, it should contain an element of forward thinking and forestalling, and should not be used as a synonym for *expect*, which is a perfectly good word to use instead:

✓ *I cannot entirely **anticipate** [= think forward to] what will happen.*

✓ *The changes **anticipated** [= looked forward to] the annual reshuffle due in September.*
✗ *The RUC did not **anticipate** [✓ expect] any trouble.*
✗ *It had been great fun, much more so than he had **anticipated** [✓ expected].*

If you can replace *anticipate* with *expect* and still get the same meaning, use *expect*.

apt / liable / prone

*Majorities are always **apt to** forget that in another context they might constitute a minority.*
*The debate is **apt to** collapse into gross oversimplification.*
*Items like heating and lighting are **liable to** be costlier.*
*The blooms are **prone to** rot in wet weather.*

When followed by a *to*-infinitive, as in the examples above, *apt*, *liable*, and *prone* are virtually interchangeable, although *prone* and *liable* tend to imply disapproval and *liable* has stronger connotations of responsibility.

Liable also has a special role in the context of legal obligation:

*Anyone who aids the commission of an offence is **liable to** be tried and punished in the same way.*
*The register is a list of those **liable to** pay the charge.*

Unlike *apt to*, *liable to* and *prone to* can be followed by a simple noun object instead of a *to*-clause:

*The affected children are **liable to** behavioural problems.*
*This method is also **liable to** abuse.*
*Luxury goods would remain **liable to** duty.*

*He was **prone to** lapses of memory after a binge.*
*Older patients are especially **prone to** accidents in a general hospital.*
*The slopes of the Marne valley are particularly **prone to** frost.*

Bear in mind that *likely to* is a better choice in the context of a particular or immediate probability:

*American holidaymakers are **likely to** be more at risk than British ones.*
*Domestic prices were **likely to** remain high until new supplies arrived.*

assume / presume

Both words can be used with a simple object, a *that*-clause (or one with *that* omitted), or an object followed by a *to*-infinitive:

*Don't **assume** that questions will be worded in the same way every year.*
*'Now,' murmured Benjamin, 'let's **assume** I am the assassin.'*
*These incomers were **presumed** to be somewhat different.*

These words are largely interchangeable in the meaning 'suppose', although some have proposed the distinction that *assume* tends to state a hypothesis whereas *presume* tends to draw a conclusion from evidence:

*I noticed your door was half open. I **presume** you were inside.*
*We **presume** that we are doing something wrong when we do not achieve immediate results.*

avenge / revenge

You *avenge* someone (including yourself) for a wrong or suffering, or you avenge the act itself.

*Their programme was to **avenge** themselves for their injuries by harrying the king's country.*
*The Trojans wish to **avenge** the death of Hector.*
*A hobgoblin would **avenge** himself for any insult by stealing all the family's keys.*

But you *revenge* only an act or yourself:

*The dwarfs saw their chance to **revenge** themselves and pre-pared a trap for the retreating Orc army.*
*Someone's drunken wife might decide to **revenge** herself on her husband.*

Revenge is much more common as a noun, and *to take* (or *seek*) *revenge on* (or *for*) is a convenient catch-all idiom available to cover most of the cases mentioned:

*The Americans must have felt he **was taking revenge on** them for what had happened.*
*They say Mrs Aquino **is seeking revenge for** the murder of her husband.*

> *He was not a double first, nor even a first class man; but he revenged himself on the university by putting firsts and double firsts out of fashion for the year, and laughing down a species of pedantry which at the age of twenty-three leaves no room in a man's mind for graver subjects than conic sections or Greek accents.*
>
> Anthony Trollope, *Barchester Towers*, 1857

backward / backwards *and related words*

In British English *backward* is more usual when it is an adjective (as in a *backward glance*), and *backwards* when it is an adverb (as in *walking backwards*). The same distinction between *-ward* and *-wards* applies to related words, such as *forward(s)* and *homeward(s)* and the compass directions *eastward(s)*, *northward(s)*, *southward(s)*, and *westward(s)*.

*Some insects are also capable of **backward** flight.*
*It was snowing on the day we resumed our **northward** journey.*
*We shuddered back across the waves towards a weary **homeward** haul.*
*The algorithm needs to scan **backwards** as well as **forwards**.*
*The torso is capable of twists and bends in any direction at the waist: **forwards**, sideways, and **backwards**.*
*He hummed to himself as they continued **northwards**.*
*Descent is made **southwards** over a pathless moor.*
*Packs of youngsters on bicycles were streaming **homewards** for their midday meal.*

Adverb forms in *-ward* are more common in American English and are also found in British:

*It should not matter whether time is running **backward** or **forward**.*
*Let us start with Rome and speed **northward**.*
*She turned and made her way **homeward**.*

It is best to avoid the inconsistency found in the following example taken from actual usage:

*? You can go **forward** and **backwards** on the back and your hands are free to play.*

barely / hardly / scarcely

These limiting adverbs are all used more or less inter-changeably with adjectives and verbs:

*The light **barely** filtered through.*
*The voice was **barely** audible above the noise of the traffic.*
***Hardly** anyone present could understand a word.*
*Alyssia **hardly** dared look at him.*
*There could **scarcely** be a less promising environment for an amphibian than the desert of central Australia.*
*They are **scarcely** adult, some men.*

If there is a continuation this should be introduced by a time word such as *when* or *before* and not *than* (and note the inversion in the third example):

*Bruce **scarcely** bothered to hide the murder in his eyes **when** he caught the king's glance.*
*The two women had **barely** crossed the threshold **before** they were halted in their tracks.*
***Hardly** had Western European leaders accepted the proposals **when** Carter changed his mind.*

basis *(as in* on a daily basis*)*

The phrase *on a – basis* can be a useful one:

Awards may be held on either a full-time or a part-time basis.

This is more precise than saying, for example, *awards may be held either full-time or part-time*. But simple adverbs of time will often serve just as well:

? *They will hope that their child can go to school **on a daily basis** from home like his fully sighted peers.*

(✓ . . . *can go to school* ***daily*** *or* ***every day*** . . .)

? *The fact of being 'family' is no guarantee that people can live happily together* ***on a long-term basis***.

(✓ . . . *can live together* ***long-term*** *or* ***indefinitely*** . . .)

beg the question

This is a common expression that is used incorrectly more often than correctly. It properly means 'to assume as true what the argument is setting out to prove to be true':

It ***begs the question*** *to assume that if penalties were harsher violent crimes would decrease.*

It is widely used in two incorrect meanings for which good alternatives are available:

- 'to suggest or give rise to the question':

✗ *Asking if the government should pay of course* ***begs the question*** *[✓ raises the question], where does the government get the cash from.*

✗ *The imminent introduction of digital television and its 200 channels* ***begs a question*** *[✓ brings a question to mind or makes me wonder]. When I have found space for my wide-screen TV, my VCR and various set-top boxes with the obligatory three miles of cable and plugs . . . where do I sit?*

- 'to evade the issue; to duck the question':

✗ *The debate has been sterile because each side* ***has begged the question*** *[✓ evaded the issue] by assuming itself to be correct.*

behalf: on behalf of

On behalf of means 'in the interests of' or 'for the benefit of' or 'as a representative of':

✓ *It is for the government to regulate **on behalf of** [= in the interests of] the community.*
✓ *Let the children have a say on what is bought **on their behalf** [= for their benefit].*
✓ *I am delighted to accept this award **on behalf of** [= as representative of] the department.*
✓ *Would you apologize to Steve **on our behalf** [= as our representative].*

It should not be used to mean 'on the part of':

✗ *The problem arose from carelessness on their behalf [✓ on their part].*
✗ *There is a lot of new interest generated on behalf of [✓ on the part of, by] journalists.*

between / among

The view that *between* can only be used when two people or things are involved is a language superstition, probably derived from the use of *between* in relation to physical measurement and distance. But its use with reference to more than two things is common and often preferable to the proposed alternative *among* (or *amongst*: see the entry for these words on p. 219):

*Assessment should be seen as a partnership **between** teachers, other professionals, and parents.*
*On the journey I heard snatches of conversation **between** my guards.*

*The company has taken on ten extra staff to make up the order, and **between** them they are turning out more than 300 puppets a day.*
*Does he sigh **between** the chimes of the clock?*

blatant / flagrant

Blatant was coined by the poet Spenser at the end of the 16th century, and means 'completely obvious or conspicuous', normally with reference to things disapproved of:

*The general population has no stomach for such **blatant** bigotry.*
*I reckon this could be a **blatant** attempt to influence a police officer in the execution of his duty.*
*When Harry Met Sally was thought too **blatant** [= sexually explicit] for normal TV viewing.*
*'Sorry,' he drawled with **blatant** insincerity.*

Flagrant is an older word with a generally similar meaning, but its emphasis is much more on the offensiveness or shockingness of the act it describes than on the obviousness:

*His subjects thought him guilty of a **flagrant** breach of the promises made by the Charter.*
*It is difficult to see how this could ever be achieved without a **flagrant** disregard for basic human rights.*
*The flights were **flagrant** violations of the no-fly zone.*
*The ill-doings of his associates became so **flagrant** that protests from England brought about a fatal confrontation.*

Except in casual conversation, it is best to avoid using the adverb *blatantly* in its more recent weakened meaning equivalent to 'absolutely' or 'extremely'.

both / both of

Both can be used as a modifier or as a kind of pronoun followed by *of*; the first choice tends to emphasize the collective nature of the combination and the second choice the individuality of each:

*The majority of children under 16 live with **both** their natural parents.*
*She went into the kitchen and made coffee for **both of** us. (Or you could say: . . . for us both.)*
*They **both** seem remarkably cheerful.*
***Both** girls laughed. To them 40 seemed positively ancient.*

There are a few traps for the unwary in using the word *both*. In the following sentence, a moment's reflection will show the illogical nature of the statement:

? *There is a house on both sides of the road.*

There is nothing grammatically wrong with this but it is clearly counter-intuitive in referring to one house on two sides of the road, since a single house can only be in one place. This sentence therefore needs either to be put more consistently in the plural or to be recast with *each* instead of *both*:

? *There are houses on both sides of the road.* (But this doesn't make it clear that there are only two.)
✓ *There is a house on each side of the road.* (Success!)

both . . . and . . .

As an adverb, *both* should be paired with *and* and not *or*, and it is important to balance the two parts of the structure:

*The sample comprised **both** single **and** married women.*
*My move from accountancy to law will be **both** a challenge **and** a change of emphasis.*
*Anthropology **both** masked **and** revealed Eliot's own concerns.*

In the following sentences the two parts of the *both . . . and . . .* structure are inconsistent:

✗ *Only seven countries in the world can claim to be **both** homogeneous **and** to have no border problems.*
(Reorder as ✓ *. . . claim **both** to be homogeneous **and** to have no border problems . . .*)

✗ *This applies **both** to the boys **and** the girls.*
(There needs to be another *to* after *and* to balance the first *to*: ✓ *This applies both to the boys and to the girls.* Alternatively, make the first *to* govern the two parts: ✓ *This applies to both the boys and the girls.*)

✗ *Her speech was **both** detrimental to understanding and to peace.*
(As constructed here, we expect another adjective after *and* to balance *detrimental*, e.g. ✓ *Her speech was **both** detrimental to understanding **and** damaging to peace.* As it stands, the order should be ✓ *Her speech was detrimental **both to** understanding **and to** peace* or ✓ *Her speech was detrimental to **both** understanding **and** peace.*)

compare with / to

You may be unsure about which word follows *compare*: *to* or *with*. The choice can cause a lot of doubt, but there is a fairly simple rule you can apply to your writing. If the comparison tends to liken two people or things, use *to*, whereas if it tends to weigh or balance one thing against another and find differences, use *with*.

- balancing one against another, seeking differences:

*Then there were only 1.7 million vehicles on the road **compared with** around 24.5 million now.*
*These values **were compared with** findings in ten control experiments.*
*Chesterfield's range of occupations was limited when **compared with** what was on offer in Worcester, Leicester, or York.*

- likening or seeking resemblance:

*Mr Wilson **compared** his role as Prime Minister at various times **to** a 'soccer midfield sweeper'.*
*It has also been suggested that rape in marriage cannot **be compared** to other forms of rape.*

In the following examples, *to* needs to be replaced by *with* and vice versa:

*If you want to upgrade your RAM you'll have to unplug these, but that's nothing **compared to** the headache of removing a disk drive. (The two processes are being contrasted, not likened.)*
*They were constantly **comparing** their own beliefs **with** Greek*

beliefs, trying to find support for them. (The beliefs are being likened, not contrasted.)

> *Perhaps, there is no man in the world, of my birth,*
> *whose misfortunes can at all be compared to mine.*

Thackeray, *The Memoirs of Barry Lyndon*, 1856

comprise / compose / consist of / constitute

Comprise, compose, consist, and *constitute* are all used to describe how a whole is made up of its parts, but they look at the equation from different ends. *Comprise* has the whole as its grammatical subject and the parts as its grammatical object:

*The hotel's accommodation **comprises** bungalows and cottages, all facing the sea.*
*The subcommittee **comprises** six experienced bureau managers from the area.*
*The recordings **comprised** performances of opera overtures.*

Consist of takes the same perspective, and so the first of these sentences could also be expressed as follows with the same meaning:

*The hotel's accommodation **consists of** bungalows and cottages, all facing the sea.* (An alternative is *include*, but this might imply other elements not mentioned.)

It is, however, incorrect to use *comprise* with opposite reference, starting with the parts and leading to the whole:

✗ *Bungalows and cottages **comprise** the hotel's accommodation.*

✗ *Nationalist elements **comprised** the major part of the resistance forces.*

In these cases, the verb to use is *constitute* or *compose*:

✓ *Bungalows and cottages **constitute** the hotel's accommodation.*

✓ *Nationalist elements **constituted** the major part of the resistance forces.*

✓ *Proteins **compose** much of the actual substance of the human body.* (You could also use a more general word such as *form* or *make up*.)

Even worse is to use *comprise* in a hybrid passive construction *be comprised of*:

✗ *We can characterize the human body as a system which **is comprised of** a number of subsystems.*

✗ *The cargo **was comprised of** junked vehicles, pipes, tanks, and drilling rig components.*

Here, the verb to use is *consist of*:

✓ *We can characterize the human body as a system which **consists of** a number of subsystems.*

✓ *The cargo **consisted of** junked vehicles, pipes, tanks, and drilling rig components.*

consider as

There are three possible constructions for *consider* in its meaning 'to regard as being'. The first two are straightforward but the third is more controversial:

• with a simple object followed by a noun or adjective in grammatical agreement with it:

*If Rupert had not been a bear, he might have been **considered** prissy, like Noddy.*
*What would you **consider** justifiable reasons for going into debt?*

• with a simple object followed by a *to*-infinitive:

*I **consider** him **to be** one of my closest friends.*
*There is a stylish restaurant overlooking the garden, **considered to have** one of the best chefs in Garda.*

• followed by *as*, on the analogy of words such as *regard* and *treat*:

*State pensions are **considered as** earned income for tax purposes.*

continuous / continual

*The urgent need for cash is a **continuous** [= continuing] threat to the initiative.*
*This work was beset by **continual** [= repeated] interruptions.*

These words are often confused: usually, *continual* is used where *continuous* is needed. *Continuous* means 'continuing without interruption', whereas *continual* means 'recurring repeatedly'. So a continuous noise goes on all the time, like a hum or drone or babble, but continual noises come and go at intervals, like heavy vehicles passing in the street outside. (For this reasons, *continual* is more often found with plurals.)

The same distinction applies to the adverbs *continually* and *continuously*:

*Water poured **continuously** [= without interruption] from a high-level tank.*
*They were discussing a machine that was **continually** [= repeatedly] breaking down.*

correspond to / with

*The title lecturer **corresponds** roughly **to** assistant professor in North American usage.*
*Students then ticked the boxed word or phrase which **corresponds to** the sentence they think they heard.*
*We want a major presence that **corresponds to** the size of that market.*

With one exception, you can normally use either *to* or *with* after *correspond*, but *with* implies a stronger element of agreement or conformity rather than straightforward similarity or analogy:

*There's not a single track on the disc that **corresponds with** the list in the sleeve note.*
*The terminal checks with the bank's computer that the number **corresponds with** the card.*
*The distribution of the hoards does not **correspond with** either population or wealth.*

The exception is the meaning 'to exchange letters', which requires *with*:

*The two friends continued to **correspond with** one another after the war.*

criteria

Criteria, meaning 'principles by which something is judged', is a plural noun, the singular form being *criterion*:

*Non-academic **criteria** have a clear priority over the academic.*
*There are several **criteria** to look for when choosing a food supplement for your horse.*

Because the plural form is used so much more frequently than the singular, it has taken on the role of a singular noun with a corresponding grammatical construction:

✗ *The proposed increases don't quite meet that [✓ those] **criteria**.*

Unlike *data*, *agenda*, and other words that have largely changed from plural to singular, *criteria* cannot be justified as a singular mass noun, because it refers to several items rather than a group of items.

cupful / cupfuls *and related words*

*That's three **cupfuls** you've drunk.*
*She was in the habit of crunching large **handfuls** of crisps.*
*Cook all the mixture a few **spoonfuls** at a time.*

The plural forms of nouns ending in *-ful* when used as a measure are *cupfuls*, *handfuls*, etc., and not *cupsful*, *handsful*, etc. But when the reference is to actual cups and hands being full, each word retains its separate identity. *Three cupfuls* are an amount measured in terms of a cup, whereas *three cups full of water* are actual cups containing water; similarly there is a distinction between *he was carrying a handful of paper clips* and *he had his hands full of paper clips*.

Other words of this type are *carful, earful, eyeful, forkful, spoonful* (and derivatives such as *tablespoonful, teaspoonful*, etc.), and *tankful*.

Adjectives ending in *-ful*, such as *beautiful, careful, faithful, graceful, harmful, lawful, merciful, skilful*, and *thankful*, obviously do not have plurals, but they form adverbs in *-fully* (*beautifully, carefully, faithfully, gracefully, harmfully, lawfully, mercifully, skilfully, thankfully*, etc.).

dare *and* need

*The landlady **need** never know.*
*He doesn't know if he **dare** trust her.*

These examples illustrate the unusual behaviour of two special verbs, *dare* and *need*. Normally, we would expect a verb in the third person singular of the present tense (i.e. after *he, she, it*, or a singular noun) to end in *-s*, as in *the landlady cooks our meals*.

Dare and *need* are called **semi-modal** verbs because they behave in some ways (but not all) like the **modal** verbs including *can, may, might, must, should*, and *will*. These verbs too have the same form in all their persons, including the third person singular: *I **can** come, you **can** come, he **can** come*, etc. In addition, they form negatives and questions without needing the help of *do*: *I **will** not come, you **must** not delay, **should** I answer the letter? Dare* and *need* share all these features in some of their uses.

These special uses of *dare* and *need* are restricted to particular grammatical contexts. All these are most noticeable in the third person singular (after *he, she, it,* etc.), because then *dare* and *need* do not end in -*s* and so the difference is more obvious:

- after conjunctions such as *because, how, if, whether,* etc.:

*He only hates because he **dare not** love.*
*I don't know how you **dare** show your face.*
*We're not sure if we **need** apply.*

- in negative constructions (with *not, never,* etc.):

*I **dare not** admit it.*
*You **need not** stay any longer.*
*We **never need** go there again.*

- in questions:

*The house is – **dare I** say it? – homely.*
***Need** we remind you of your duty?*
*How **dare you** say that?* (This is also used as an exclamation, and is the most common use of *dare* in this form of question.)

Dare and *need* also form contracted negative forms *daren't* and *needn't*, on the analogy of *can't, mayn't, mustn't, shouldn't,* etc.

Notice that *dare not* and *need not* (and their contracted forms *daren't* and *needn't*) do not use *to* before a following infinitive: *you need not stay*, not *you need not to stay* (which could be taken to mean 'you must not stay', i.e. 'you have to leave'). The same applies when *dare* and *need* form questions without *do*: *dare I say it?*, not *dare I to say it?*

But the really odd thing about *dare* and *need* is that, in addition to these modal functions, they can also be used as ordinary verbs conforming to the normal rules of inflection and grammar (this is why they are called *semi*-modals):

*He can come if he **dares**.*
*She **did not dare** (to) say any more.*
***Does** your room **need** cleaning?*
*You **don't need** to pay yet.*

And the three earlier sentences could be rewritten in the same way:

*You **do not** (or **don't**) **need** to stay any longer.*
*He only hates because he **does not dare** (to) love.*

In these uses, *dare* and *need* change to *dares* and *needs* in the third person singular, *to* is optional with *dare* and obligatory with *need* before a following infinitive, and they are supported by *do* in questions and negative statements.

In the past tenses, *dare* tends to be supported by *do* or *have* to form negatives and questions, although it can also be used in direct negatives without *do*:

*She **did not dare** (to) stop or rest.*
*They **dared not** continue.*
*I **haven't dared** (to) see the doctor yet.*

But *need* in the past tenses is always supported by *do* or *have* to form negatives and questions:

*You **didn't need** to do that.*

How then do you choose between these alternative patterns, when there is a choice? The choice is limited to the grammatical contexts noted above, i.e. the third person singular, negative constructions, and questions. It is largely a matter of style and personal preference, but you may have noticed that the semi-modal patterns are rather more rhetorical, i.e. they make a stronger point, whereas in their normal behaviour the two verbs are rather more matter-of-fact. But this is only a guideline, not a hard-and-fast rule. It's a good idea to look out for these uses in your reading, and note the effect that writers' choices make on their writing.

One small warning: it is important to avoid mixing the two patterns, e.g. to use the *dares* form with a direct negative, which is only possible with the *dare* form:

✗ *He only hates because he **dares not** love.*
✓ *He only hates because he **dare not** love.*

different *from / to / than*

The adjective *different* can be followed by three linking words: *from*, *to*, and *than*. Of these, the only one that everyone accepts is *from*:

*A mosaic of minor communities, many of them strikingly **different from** one another.*
*Looking after a pregnant teenager is obviously **different from** fostering a small child.*

The argument runs that because we say that one thing *differs from* another, we should say that one thing is *different from* another. But English does not always work as logically as this. For example, we say *accord with* but *according to*. In actual use, as distinct from the theory, *different* is followed by *to* as often as it is by *from*:

*The new courts are no **different to** the ones they replace.*

It is less often followed by *than*, which is more common in American English:

*Their obsession may seem no **different than** the fanaticism of collectors of rare books or woodblock prints.*

It is tempting to use *than* when a clause follows, although it can often be rephrased:

*? She is very **different** now **than** she was five years ago.*
*✓ She is very **different from what** she was five years ago.*

There are occasions when *from* is inelegant and *to* or even *than* is more natural, especially when *different* is separated from the continuation it relates to:

*✓ The attitude of the players is so **different** now **to** what it was a year ago.*
*✓ I found that a meadow seen against the light was an entirely **different** tone of green **to** the same meadow facing the light.*
*✓ Spirituality is a genuinely **different** dimension **to** reality.*
*✓ A false sense of security which makes drivers behave quite **differently** on motorways **than** on ordinary roads.*

dilemma

Dilemma has a special meaning; it is more than a mere synonym for 'difficulty' or 'difficult choice'. A dilemma is indeed a difficult choice, but it is more than this: it is a choice between two alternatives both of which are bad or unpleasant, so that the choice, whichever way it is made, cannot be a good or positive one:

*When I was a little lad I always thought that the **dilemma** to be or not to be had something to do with choosing pencils.*

This example, flippant though it is, shows a good use of *dilemma*, because Shakespeare's Hamlet was indeed faced with a dilemma when he made his famous speech.

In the following examples, one or both of the available choices is a good one, or the choices are unexpressed or undefined, so that the use of *dilemma* is questionable:

? *Faced with the **dilemma** [✓ choice or problem] of what would be best for her four young children, Nikki had considered trying to find someone to temporarily look after them.*
? *The **dilemma** [✓ conflict] between the requirement of maintaining an attractive village landscape and the provision of housing for those in need has become more acute.*

As a rule of thumb, if you can substitute words such as *choice, decision, difficulty*, or any of those given above without compromising the intended meaning, you are safer using them.

disinterested / uninterested

Problems often lie in the history of words, and here is a *cause célèbre* illustrating this. These words relate to different meanings of the word *interest*. Both words used to have the same meaning, which is that corresponding to *uninterested* in modern use, i.e. 'lacking interest' where the sense of *interest* is 'readiness to be concerned with someone or something':

*Although **uninterested** in politics, he became chairman of the local defence committee when terrorists began attacking the farms.*

*Apoplectic businessmen raged at **uninterested** airline staff about how it was vital that they attended some meeting.*

From the 17th century, however, *disinterested* acquired a meaning 'impartial, unbiased', which relates to another meaning of *interest*, 'personal advantage or involvement':

*The analysis shows the ideal of the **disinterested** administrator carrying out the orders of his political masters.*

*He was persuaded by friends that he had still much to offer by way of **disinterested** advice to younger colleagues.*

*Not everybody believed that his outrage on their behalf was **disinterested**.*

This distinction in usage is supported by many, who find it useful, although alternative words are available for *disinterested* in both meanings: *uninterested* in one and *impartial*, *unbiased*, and *detached* for the other. (There is also *unconcerned*, but this too can involve an ambiguity based on the varying meanings of *concern*.)

In more recent use, *disinterested* has controversially begun to revert to its older meaning, coinciding with *uninterested* and sharing its use of *in*:

✗ *The crocodiles have become fat and **disinterested** in [✓ uninterested in or indifferent to] sex during the spring mating season.*

✗ *He'd been so **disinterested** [✓ uninterested or unconcerned] in her progress during six years of primary school that he'd only ever visited the school once.*

In these sentences, the more straightforward word *uninterested* can be substituted harmlessly, and this is the best course since use of *disinterested* in this meaning is widely disliked, frequent though it is.

> *'It's likely to be a very cheap funeral,' said the same speaker; 'for upon my life I don't know of anybody to go to it. Suppose we make up a party and volunteer?' 'I don't mind going if a lunch is provided,' observed the gentleman with the excrescence on his nose. 'But I must be fed, if I make one.' Another laugh. 'Well, I am the most disinterested among you, after all,' said the first speaker, 'for I never wear black gloves, and I never eat lunch.'*
>
> Charles Dickens, *A Christmas Carol*, 1843

doubt if / whether / that

When *doubt* is used to mean 'to think something unlikely', the standard link words with what follows (the object of the doubt) are *if* and *whether*, and the same applies when *doubt* is a noun in phrases such as *there is doubt*:

*I **doubt if** a statement next week would be appropriate.*
*I **doubt if** I have a single drop of aristocratic blood in my veins.*
*There must be **doubt whether** Dickens himself held any firm belief in the afterlife.*
*She **doubts whether** the Chancellor will offer any long-term solutions.*

When *doubt* is used in the negative (with *no*, *not*, etc.) to mean, in effect, 'it is likely', the link word is normally *that*:

*There's no **doubt that** sex gets your heart going.*
*No one can **doubt that** it is better to try to prevent job problems arising in the first place.*

As usual, the *that* of the *that*-clause can be omitted:

*No one **doubts** he has earned his place among the sport's leading players.*
*I don't **doubt** there was something really wrong with him.*
*Nor can he **doubt** the assault was attempted murder.*

The logical basis for this distinction lies in the nature and implications of doubting. When *doubt* is grammatically positive its meaning suggests uncertainty in the following clause (for which *if* and *whether* are more suitable) whereas not doubting, which is grammatically negative, is conceptually positive, making a *that*-clause more logical. For this reason, many people dislike the increasing use of a *that*-clause after a use of *doubt* in the affirmative:

? *I **doubt that** the book will be of any use to the professional.*
? *There have been many **doubts that** he couldn't make a comeback at club level.*
? *He **doubted** Ferrari would sue him.*

Although this usage is widely regarded as an American-ism, it is in fact found in British English from the end of the 19th century and is now common. It is as well, however, to be aware that it is controversial.

due to

*The **richness of this collection** is entirely due to the generosity and collecting mania of one man.*
*Eimer argued that **the similarities** were due to an entirely different cause.*

This innocent-looking little phrase causes a great deal of bother. It consists of the adjective *due* and the preposition *to*, and together they form what is known as a prepositional phrase (i.e. a phrase having the role of a preposition, as in *due to the rain*). Strictly speaking, because *due* is an adjective, it needs a specific antecedent noun or noun phrase it can refer to. In each of the sentences given above, *due to* has an antecedent shown in bold.

No one objects to this type of use, but you will find a lot of resistance to the use of *due to* without such a clear noun-type antecedent:

? *Outdoor tomatoes were an amazing success in many parts of the country last year **due to** the hot summer.*
? *Our rugby has deteriorated **due to** the way it has been managed.*

In these sentences, we have to supply a linking phrase such as 'and this is/was' or 'and this fact is/was' before *due to* to make the grammar work in a way that satisfies everyone:

✓ *Outdoor tomatoes were an amazing success in many parts of the country last year, **and this was due to** the hot summer.*
✓ *Our rugby has deteriorated, **and this fact is due to** the way it has been managed.*

When you would have to do this to complete the grammar, it is usually better to use an alternative such as *owing to* or *because of*, which are structurally freer of the preceding part of the sentence:

✓ *Outdoor tomatoes were an amazing success in many parts of the country last year **owing to** the hot summer.*
✓ *Our rugby has deteriorated **because of** the way it has been managed.*

To complete the picture, note that *due* and *to* can come together with a different meaning, when *due* means 'required or expected' and *to* introduces a following infinitive, in which case a noun or pronoun antecedent always occurs:

*The car was found less than 100 yards from the sports centre where she was **due to** take a class.*

economic / economical

Pairs of adjectives ending in *-ic* and *-ical* cause problems of differentiation: others are *classic/classical*, *comic/comical*, and *historic/historical*. The underlying reason is that the meanings within each pair overlap. For some reason the pair *economic/economical* seems to cause particular problems.

As is often the case with words of this type, the form in *-ic* is the basic one meaning 'to do with economics' or 'in terms of the economy' (in its sense 'the structure of financial organization in a country'):

*There were finally some signs of **economic** recovery.*
*Their skills have yet to be tested in a tougher **economic** climate.*

It also has the meaning 'efficient and profitable':

*It is not **economic** to run both centres any more.*
*Villas can be an **economic** option for families wanting to share accommodation.*

The form in *-ical* tends to mean 'providing or practising economy' (in the sense 'value for money') with 'economy' being interpreted fairly broadly (e.g. economy of movement as well as financial economy, and remember the resonant phrase *economical with the truth*):

*The system is cheap to set up and **economical** to run.*
*Many parents tend to be **economical** in the use of attention or praise.*
*The taut muscles in the arms and thighs were revealed by his **economical** movements.*

In some sentences, you can see the difference in meaning if you substitute one word for the other:

*The railways should provide very **economic** [= profitable] transport.*
*The railways should provide very **economical** [= inexpensive] transport.*

enormity

Enormity is a commonly misused word: misused because it has a special meaning that is usefully preserved. It means properly 'great wickedness' or 'a wicked or terrible' act, and it is wasted as a mere substitute for *enormousness* (in the simpler sense 'great size'):

✓ Perhaps the **enormity** of what he was doing got to him.

✓ The **enormities** of the Hitler regime and the Holocaust have been the subject of many psychological studies.

✗ A wide-angle lens captures the **enormity** of the building.

✗ He felt drained, shattered by the **enormity** of all he had learned.

Admittedly, *enormousness* is an ungainly mouthful of letters, and this may be why the more elegant word *enormity* is trying to take it over, but there are other alternatives that cut the Gordian knot effectively, such as *hugeness*, *immensity*, *magnitude*, or *vastness*, or phrases such as *huge* (or *great*) *size* or *vast dimensions* (or *scale*). Another option is to recast the sentence more widely, for example:

✓ He felt drained, shattered by all (or *how much*) he had learned.

equally as

You can normally just say *equally* in comparisons like the following:

? There were men **equally as** bright and considerably younger.
? Other facts are **equally as** impressive.

✓ There were men **equally** bright and considerably younger.
✓ Other facts are **equally** impressive.

A useful and often less awkward alternative is *just as*:

✓ There were men **just as** bright and considerably younger.
✓ Other facts are **just as** impressive.

especially / specially

Take care not to use the wrong word inadvertently, as this is all too easy. *Especially* means 'more than in other cases':

*He would pray for her family, and **especially** for her.*

Whereas *specially* means 'for a special purpose':

*Pesticide tests need to be developed **specially** for hot countries.*

The mistake often made is that *especially* is used where *specially* is called for:

✗ *These garments are created **especially** for the wearer.*
✓ *These garments are created **specially** for the wearer.*

farther / further *and* farthest / furthest

Further and *furthest* are the older (Anglo-Saxon) forms and are also the ones in more common use today. *Farther* and *farthest* tend to be used as alternatives when the reference is to physical distance, perhaps because of their apparent closeness to the word *far*, although they are only coincidentally related to it and not derived from it:

***Farther** down the coast we saw a huge kittiwake colony.*
*On the same side of the road, some hundred yards **farther** south, stood a small cottage.*
*In a **farther** reach of the bay, the seafront lights came on.*

*The police car was discreetly parked in the **farthest** corner of the courtyard.*

*At Joppa he embarked on a boat to the **farthest** end of the known world.*
*The servants' attic bedrooms were both smallest and **farthest** from the front door.*

Further or *furthest* could be substituted in all the above examples, and in the examples that follow, which are of non-physical uses in which the sense is of degree rather than distance, this is much the more common choice:

*Her conjectures could not have been **further** from the truth.*
*Competition was **further** boosted with the lifting of exchange controls.*
*It was in Germany that the industrial complex was **furthest** developed.*

Further is the only choice in certain contexts:

• when it is an adjective meaning 'additional', as in the following examples:

*If you are interested in joining a team, call for **further** details.*
*Below are some **further** items of equipment shown at the exhibition.*
*He was told to report to the police station for **further** questioning.*

• when it is an adverb meaning 'additionally, for a longer time':

*It is unnecessary to consider **further** any of the other grounds of appeal which do not arise.*

• when it is a sentence adverb meaning 'moreover' or 'what is more':

Further, interest rates will have to rise in the new year.

• when it is a verb meaning 'to promote or advance an idea, scheme, etc.':

*They create a totally false brand of patriotism in order **to further** a particular cause.*

feasible

Feasible has a narrower range of meaning than *possible*, for which it is often used as an alternative. *Possible* can mean either 'capable of being done' (referring to practicality) or 'likely' (referring to expected outcome), whereas *feasible* properly corresponds only to the first of these meanings, 'capable of being done or carried out' or 'practical':

✓ *It would not be politically **feasible** to scrap the battle-scarred regiments after the deaths of soldiers in Iraq.*
✓ *A structural engineer found the stone walls were too dilapidated to be repaired economically and planners have accepted that demolition is the only **feasible** solution.*

It should not be used as an alternative to *possible* when it means 'likely' or 'probable':

✗ *It's quite **feasible** [✓ likely or probable] that she knew Greg.*
✗ *The Celtic manager will instruct his side to chase the game so long as a surprise result remains **feasible** [✓ possible].*

The same applies to the adverb *feasibly*, which properly means 'in a way that is practical' (a meaning also shared by *possibly*) and is not a substitute for *possibly* in its sense 'likely':

✓ *Pooling different types of skill may expand the set of projects that can **feasibly** be done.*

✗ *There's one way in which the government could **feasibly** [✓ possibly or reasonably] have been tougher.*

> *Miss Crawford's attention was first called from Fanny by Tom Bertram's telling her, with infinite regret, that he found it absolutely impossible for him to undertake the part of Anhalt in addition to the Butler; he had been most anxiously trying to make it out to be feasible, but it would not do, he must give it up.*
>
> Jane Austen, *Mansfield Park*, 1814

flat / flatly

The main adverb from *flat* is *flatly*, but it is used only in two figurative meanings, the first more common than the second:

• 'completely, without reservation' to intensify words denoting denial, refusal, rejection, contradiction, and suchlike:

*The firm **flatly** denied that there had been any problem.*
*The shopping trip ends in disaster when Brenda picks an outfit that Sandra **flatly** refuses to wear.*
*Many PR executives **flatly** reject the idea that any of the work they do could be handled from a distance.*
*This information **flatly** contradicted the novelist's own version of his life.*

• 'in a dull way' with reporting verbs such as *say*, *speak*, *inform*, and so on:

*Miss Tita gave me this information **flatly**, without any expression.*

Flat has a role halfway between adjective and adverb, but more the first than the second, when it means 'in a flat position':

*The mirror was placed **flat** against the wall.*

Flat is used as an adverb in a few fixed expressions such as *flat broke*, *flat out*, and *to turn something down flat*:

*He went **flat out** for the green.*
*Mary recalls how they were **flat broke** and living from hand to mouth.*
*A few of us **turned him down flat** and he didn't like it.*

flaunt / flout

Flaunting something, usually a quality or attribute, is parading it ostentatiously:

*If you've got it, **flaunt** it. If you haven't – find a better tailor.*

Flouting is disregarding or treating with contempt. The sorts of things that are typically flouted are rules, laws, conventions, principles, expectations, and so on:

*Police are targeting heavy goods vehicles in a crackdown on drivers who are **flouting** the law.*

former *and* latter

Former and *latter*, referring respectively to the first of two people or things mentioned and to the second, can both be used either alone as nouns (usually as *the former* and *the latter*) or as modifiers (*the former person*, *the latter thing*):

*Hire purchase and finance leasing work very similarly but **the former** is becoming increasingly popular because of bigger tax advantages.*
*EU politicians will consider whether to continue long and diffi-cult negotiations with five international partners over where to build the vast trial reactor – or to draw a line under the talks and go it alone with the project. If **the latter decision** is made, the reactor could be built by the end of the decade.*

But when they appear together contrastively in the same sentence they are usually unaccompanied:

*Other titles used by hospital-based doctors – registrars and house officers – mean nothing to patients. What registers do **the former** keep and which houses do **the latter** inhabit?*

Former and *latter* should not be used in this way when more than two items have been mentioned:

✗ *It seems reasonable to conjecture that these conditions foster child neglect, abuse, and even infanticide. **The latter** [✓ The last or This last] was, for instance, a commonly applied solution to unwanted births in the 19th century.*

Nor is it a good idea to use *former* or *latter* when the items they refer to are ill-defined or positioned a long way back in the sentence, making it difficult for the reader to make the link without a lot of unwelcome backtracking:

? *John Tavener's music is an uneasy pact between time and eternity. Compelled to exist in time, it strains and aspires to timelessness. When, in its very making, it approaches **the latter** – or at least the illusion of it – then a small miracle occurs.*

What is *the latter* here? *Eternity* is the only clearly contrasted alternative, but this occurs at the end of the previous sentence. The writer probably intended *timelessness*, which is contrasted with *time*, but this is done only implicitly, and the aside that follows be-tween dashes is an added complication. The reader has work to do to avoid confusion, and this means that the writer has failed to write effectively and clearly.

Note that both words have meanings not shared correspondingly by the other:

• *Former* has a meaning to which *latter* does not corre-spond, namely 'having been previously but no longer':

*Mrs Beckham, who is expecting her third child in March, is the only **former** Spice Girl not to have had a solo number one.*
*A transfer of property from the **former** husband to the **former** wife will come within these provisions.*
*Most of the other old names which were sold to overseas buyers – such as Flemings, Schroders and Hambros – do live on, albeit without their **former** kudos. (And note the effective use of albeit in this last example: see the entry on this word on p. 217!)*

• *Latter* has a meaning to which *former* does not corre-spond, denoting the last stage or stages of a process or the most recent part of a period of time (as in *latter-day*):

*He would need further help in the **latter** phase of the project. The old military bands no longer interest people. Possibly they have become less popular because of the summers we have experienced in **latter** years.*

fortunate / fortuitous

*It was **fortuitous** [= accidental, coincidental] that Christie's had sent the Van Gogh on a pre-auction tour of Japan. The results are based on a **fortunate** [= useful, beneficial] discovery made in 1968.*

Both words come from the Latin word *fortuna* and relate to our word *fortune*. *Fortunate* means 'having good fortune', and implies good luck or benefit, whereas *fortuitous* means 'occurring by chance' and implies mere accident or coincidence. *Fortuitous*, because of the similarity of form, is often used wrongly as though it too meant 'fortunate'. A fortuitous choice is one that is accidental or random, not one that has a good outcome, although this might also be the case: if this second meaning is the one intended, then *fortunate* is the word needed.

Follow the same distinction in the adverbs *fortuitously* and *fortunately*:

*All this happened while the principal beneficiary was **fortuitously** [= by chance] out of the room.*
***Fortunately** [= by good chance], the house was empty when the bomb exploded.*

fulsome

Although *fulsome* was originally complimentary or at least neutral in its meaning 'copious, abundant', by the 16th century it had acquired unfavourable overtones which, used correctly, it still has, suggesting excess rather than generosity:

*When Lady Macbeth welcomes Duncan, the **fulsome** insincerity of her verse is by now unmistakable to us.*

Hardly a compliment! But more recently, a more positive meaning has started to reappear:

? *Lulu gave them tea and **fulsome** [✓ profuse] apologies for not being able to remember their names.*
? *Baldwin pays **fulsome** [✓ generous] tribute to the 'quality people' around him, which naturally includes his wife.*
? *Alan Munro was understandably **fulsome** [✓ generous or lavish] in his praise of his young side.*

People will know what you mean if you follow this usage, but it will sometimes grate with them, and because the word still comes with the baggage of several hundred years of unpleasant overtones, it is best to avoid it. Alternative words include *profuse*, *lavish*, *enthusiastic*, *generous*, and *liberal*.

had rather

Sometimes, in very informal speech, *had rather* is used instead of *would rather*. This is probably because the two forms can sound much the same in the run of ordinary conversation. *Had rather* is non-standard however, and should be avoided:

✗ *I **had rather** [✓ would rather] be at the bottom of the River Thames than one week in debt.*

however

There are two points on which *however* can cause trouble:

• when to spell it as two words rather than one (as with *what ever* and *when ever*): you will find advice on this on pp. 59–61.
• whether it can come at the beginning of a sentence when it means 'on the other hand'.

The view that *however* cannot come at the beginning of a sentence is a superstition. In fact, *however* is fairly mobile within a sentence, and choice of position is usually a matter of emphasis and sentence balance. If you put it at the beginning, it will have the effect of emphasizing more strongly the contrastive nature of what follows:

However, *many attempts to bottle this smell have failed.*
However, *not being out of pocket is only one factor.*

When *however* comes at the start of a sentence, the comma that follows it (as in the two examples just given) is important: as well as indicating the pause that normally follows, it prevents ambiguity. Without the comma in the first sentence a reader might think, even if only momentarily, that you are going to say *however many attempts* in the alternative sense 'regardless of how many attempts'. In the examples that follow, notice the difference between the first (with a comma) and the second (without a comma) in each pair:

However, *the figures are calculated on a monthly and not weekly basis.*
However [= in whatever way] *the figures are calculated, on a monthly and not weekly basis they would come out better.*

However, *few houses are still heated with oil.*
However *few* [= regardless of how few] *houses are still heated with oil, they contribute to pollution.*

The ambiguity is usually only temporary, because the continuation of the sentence normally makes the meaning clear; but it can cause momentary confusion and this is avoidable.

Placed later in the sentence, *however* has a generally milder effect or (as in the third example below) the effect of identifying the point of contrast more precisely:

The crisis revealed, ***however***, *that the king's war no longer had the wholehearted support of the community.*
The more difficult issue, ***however***, *remained.*
The government, ***however*** [as opposed to other people], *attributed the delays to 'technical difficulties'.*

if and when

Any writer who uses this formula lays himself open to entirely reasonable suspicions on the part of his readers. There is the suspicion that he is a mere parrot, who cannot say part of what he has often heard without saying the rest also; there is the suspicion that he likes verbiage for its own sake; there is the suspicion that he is a timid swordsman who thinks he will be safer with a second sword in his left hand; there is the suspicion that he has merely been too lazy to make up his mind between if *and* when.

H W Fowler, *A Dictionary of Modern English Usage*, 1926

Fowler's strictures sound dated and distinctly non-PC today with their reference to sword-wielding right-handed male writers, but his advice is not quite a lost cause yet. Regard *if and when* as an avoidable cliché and you will not go far wrong, although – like most clichés – it can occasionally be useful and make a good point. The following examples should help to distinguish the useful from the redundant:

✓ *She would be able to work **if and when** she chose.* (Both words have equal force: she would be able to work if she chose, and she would be able to choose when she worked.)

? *Standards have been identified as a high priority **if and when** more funds become available.* (*If* alone would be adequate.)

? *Our only concern is **if and when** Arthur catches up with them.* (*Whether* would be better, since the possibility is open.)

? *Do something **if and when** it feels right.* (Fowler turns in his grave. Avoid prevarication and choose!)

? *If you are not ready to deal with the problem of alcohol abuse **if and when** it occurs, one day you could be faced with a crisis.* (Delete 'if and when it occurs', which adds nothing.)

immune to / from

There are two main strands of meaning with this word meaning 'free from the effects or consequences of'.

• When it refers to disease, or to some other form of harm or danger compared to this, the usual construction is *immune to*:

*Women are certainly not **immune to** the damaging effects of tobacco use.*
*Some plants are **immune to** attack because of their terpenoids.*
*Luckily, professional gardeners appear to be **immune to** the elements.*
*How do I feel about the misery I've seen? Perhaps I have spent so much time in the third world that I'm **immune to** it.*

• When it refers to some kind of obligation or liability (especially a legal one), the usual construction is *immune from*:

*Both victim and aggressor should be **immune from** moral judgement.*
*People could not be **immune from** political decisions taken at Westminster.*
*Nor was the pope **immune from** criticism.*
*The decision makes it harder for foreign officials to answer civil actions for alleged international crimes by stating that they were committed on government business and so **immune from** legal action.*

The distinction is not, however, watertight because the concepts overlap. In the papal example above, for example, we could justify using *immune to* instead of *immune from*, on the grounds that 'criticism' fits in the 'attacking' category as much as it does the 'obligation' category.

infer / imply

When you come to a conclusion, you *infer* it from evidence, perhaps something that someone has said. The evidence is making an implication and you are drawing an inference; it is *implying*, and you are *inferring*:

✓ Am I to **infer** that Laurie isn't your lover?
✓ The historian can be misled as to which was the husband and which the wife, and so **infer** the wrong family name.

✓ His letter seems to **imply** that, for some reason, students should not be allowed cars.
✓ At five, he saw his younger brother drown and the film **implies** that the guilt he felt was responsible for the dark side of his soul.

The meaning of *infer* has encroached on *imply*, as sometimes happens with two words that represent the same process from different perspectives, in this case the process of drawing conclusions. In modern use you will often find *infer* used to mean 'imply', which is a fairly recent development disliked by many because it obscures the distinction between the two sides of the thinking process outlined above:

✗ The allegation against him **inferred** [✓ *implied* or *suggested*] that he had deliberately jumped from his horse, ensuring he wouldn't finish the race.

✗ I'm not **inferring** [✓ *implying* or *suggesting*] *they are running scared at the prospect, but they're certainly not looking forward to it.*

✗ *Similar craft were discovered in North America, Iraq, Vietnam, and India. This does not* **infer** [✓ *imply* or *mean*] *that Julius Caesar and his mates flew around the globe in a Lear jet stopping off in a few disparate countries.*

In all these sentences, *imply* or *suggest* can be substituted in the meaning needed, and therefore should be.

Because the meaning of *infer* has become fuzzy, it is sometimes better to avoid it – even though you would be using it correctly – in cases where both the correct and the incorrect meaning could be understood by your readers:

? *It would be wrong to* **infer** [✓ *imply* or *suggest*] *that Curbishley is disenchanted with Charlton life.*

? *He would appear to be* **inferring** [✓ *implying* or *suggesting*] *that supporters of hunting are importing 'Rent-a-Thug'.*

ironic / ironically

The two forms *ironic* and *ironical* mean much the same, and choice between them is largely a matter of rhythm and sentence balance. Their proper meanings have to do with *irony*, the expression of an idea or thought by words that normally mean the opposite, or in a manner that normally conveys the opposite. (Dramatic irony is another aspect of this: it arises when the audience is given a significant piece of information which one or more of the participants in the drama does not know, causing dramatic tension.) To say *what a lovely day* when looking out on pouring rain is a form of irony, and the statement is ironic; to smile when you are angry is to give a look that is *ironic*:

*Her sweetly **ironic** tone seemed lost on him.*
*A slight **ironical** smile flickered round Luke's mouth.*
*The announcement was made in tones that most observers took to be **ironical**.*

In a development of this meaning, facts and circumstances are ironic when they convey the opposite of what you might expect:

*It is **ironic** that the most interesting group of pre-Romanesque churches in Europe should be in a country largely taken over by the Muslims.*
*It was **ironic** that I had to travel halfway round the globe to get to know working class men from my own back yard.*

Although questioned by some language purists, this usage is so well established, and often so difficult to distinguish from the core meaning from which it emerges, that it is acceptable, especially when the few available alternatives such as *paradoxical* or *strange* do not have the same force.

lay / lie

The forms of these words cause endless trouble because they are related in meaning and the forms themselves overlap: in particular, *lay* is the base form of one verb and the past form of another, and the participles *laid* and *lain* are constantly confused (usually with *laid* used where *lain* is needed). Take special care with phrasal verbs formed from these verbs (*lay down, lie down, lay off, lay out, lay up, lie up*, etc.), which can be extra confusing. The table below should help clarify which is which of these verbs (particular trouble spots are shown with a ✗):

lay is transitive (takes an object: *to lay an egg, to lay your head down*)

present	*lay*	*Lay the tomatoes in a circle on each plate.*
		They would need all the money they could lay their hands on.
past	*laid*	*The family laid flowers at the spot where he had died.*
		She laid (✗ lay) down her letters and stared blankly at the wall.
present participle	*laying*	*The cuckoo is infamous for laying its eggs in the nests of other birds.*
		Villagers were laying out spring wheat on the roads.
past participle (used with *be, have, has*, etc.)	*laid*	*The first track was laid in 1990.*
		The fugitives have laid a false trail.
		A set of glasses had been laid out on the table.
		The company has laid off thousands of workers.

lie is intransitive (has no object: *to lie on the bed*)

present	*lie*	*Close your eyes and **lie** in a comfortable position.*
		*Her best interests **lie** in returning home.*
past	*lay*	*Two others **lay** wounded.*
		*Their abilities **lay** elsewhere.*
present participle	*lying*	*She hated to think of his sister **lying** (✗ laying) in hospital.*
		*Death **was lying** (✗ laying) in wait for Dustin once again.*
past participle (used with *be, have, has,* etc.)	*lain*	*He'd **lain** (✗ laid) in bed night after night drifting into sleep.*
		*You've probably **lain** (✗ laid) like that with dozens of women.*
		*She **should have lain down** (✗ laid down) and had a rest.*

To complete the picture, here are the various parts of the other verb **lie**, meaning 'to be untruthful':

present	*lie*	*Did you **lie** to me?*
past	*lied*	*I **lied** and said I had seen nothing.*
present participle	*lying*	*He hated **lying** to his friends.*
past participle	*lied*	*We knew they **had lied**.*

less / fewer

five items or less? or *five items or fewer*?

The first sounds natural; the second hyper-correct and forced. Choice between *less* and *fewer* is one of the great usage trouble spots of modern times. What makes it so much worse is that dogmatic insistence on a principle leads to further confusion and can produce absurdities.

There is a general rule we can state, but it only works up to a point: *fewer* is used with plural nouns and indicates number (*fewer cars*, *fewer people*), whereas *less* is used with singular nouns and indicates amount (*less food*, *less trouble*). However, when the noun denotes an amount rather than a numerical quantity, even if it is in the plural, *less* is the more natural choice:

*We have **less** than three miles to go.*
*He had taken **less** than two weeks' sick leave in the previous year.*
*Their joint income was **less** than ten thousand that year.*
*Candidates will be invited to write fifty words or **less** on a topic of their choice.*

Note that when *less* is followed by a noun with an intervening adjective ambiguity can result:

x Less *rigid helmets were available for workers in enclosed spaces.*
? *You will end up with **less** usable material.*

In the first example, if *less* is meant to go with *helmets* rather than *rigid*, it should be changed to *fewer*:

✓ Fewer *rigid helmets were available for workers in enclosed spaces*. (In fact, *fewer helmets* is preferable even without the complication of *rigid*, because the noun is distinctly numerical in implication and *less* cannot really be justified here.)

In the second example, *less* is correct whether it applies to *usable* or to *material*, but there is still ambiguity. The sentence needs to be recast in either of two ways, depending on the meaning intended:

✓ *You will end up with less material that is usable.*
✓ *You will end up with material that is less usable.*

So, is it *five items or less*, or *five items or fewer*?

Answer: both. The first regards the five items as a total amount, and the second as a number of things. The first (with *less*) is preferable because it is more natural and idiomatic, whereas the second (with *fewer*) puts an excessive emphasis on the numerical quantity rather than the cumulative effect of the total.

like *as a conjunction*

Like is used as a preposition in the sentence *Do it like me* and as a conjunction in the sentence *Do it like I do*, where it introduces a clause with a verb (the second *do*). The first is straightforward and uncontroversial but the second is widely disliked and should be avoided. You can use *as* (or *as if* or *as though*) instead:

✗ *Like* (✓ As) *I told the foreign gentleman, there was dancing in the sitting room.*
✗ *For another second I flail **like** (✓ as if) I'm drowning.*

✗ *I glance round the hall **like** (✓ as though) I've come to change the wallpaper, 30 years late.*

literally

Let's get an uncontroversial use of *literally* out of the way first. Its innocent meaning 'in a literal sense' with reference to words and terminology causes no problems:

*How far was the information about their gods and heroes **literally** true?*

The problems start when *literally* is used in the context of idiom and metaphor.

> *Every day with me is literally another yesterday for it is exactly the same.*
>
> Alexander Pope, in a letter of 1708

> *'Lift him out,' said Squeers, after he had literally feasted his eyes in silence upon the culprit. 'Bring him in; bring him in.'*
>
> Charles Dickens, *Nicholas Nickleby*, 1839

Pope was on the verge of doing it, and if Dickens could get away with it, why shouldn't we? The offence? Using *literally* when we mean 'figuratively'. By far the most common use of this lively and entertaining adverb is as a kind of ironic intensifier within a metaphor:

*For the last few years I **literally** coined money.*

One does not of course literally *feast one's eyes* or *coin money* or do any of those strange things that have been enshrined in the imagery of English idiom. Only a curmudgeon could object to this kind of light-hearted emphasis, but beware of being comic when your effect should be serious or at least neutral in tone:

*There is **literally** no time for the players to breathe in this game.*
*You could **literally** hear the silence 50 miles away.*
*It is recommended that gamers play Campaign through first but once this has been done the world is quite **literally** your oyster from here.*

Sometimes, the image in a metaphor is really brought to life, or seems to be, and in these cases *literally* is literally appropriate:

*The look on her face **literally** stopped her breath.*
*He **literally** dropped everything and ran to greet them.*
*The complexity of variables thus introduced is almost **literally** dizzying.*
*You cannot, **literally**, move a muscle.*

As an extension of this type of use, *literally* can be effective in pointing up an idiom that is especially relevant in a particular context, usually involving a play on the words of the metaphor underlying the idiom. This is a device that is popular in newspaper reporting, where it can become forced and tedious, rather like punning headlines:

? *Velcro is indispensable as a fastening; the leisurewear industry would **literally** come apart at the seams without it.*
? *The wristband may be considered particularly advanced since it allows the wearer, **literally**, to wear his heart on his sleeve.*

? *Some bands explode on to the stage and **literally** shake their audience from start to finish.*

? *We will have to take whatever steps are necessary, particularly in terms of security and intelligence, because it's no good picking the pieces up – **literally** – afterwards.*

Even worse than this triteness is to scatter *literally* in contexts that do not involve metaphor at all, using the word as an 'I'm not kidding you' tag:

? *I have visited **literally** hundreds of schools and you can tell within a few minutes the quality of the institution.*

? *We achieved the objective **literally** within days.*

? *The problem had **literally** disappeared.*

media: *singular or plural?*

Strictly speaking, *media* in its meaning 'the organs of public news communication' is a plural noun of which the singular is *medium*. But *medium* is much less common in this meaning (although it does occur, e.g. *Radio is more versatile than any other medium*), with the result that *media* has run free and become a virtually singular mass noun, like *data*. For this reason it is often used with singular verbs and determiners (*this* and *that* instead of *these* and *those*, and so on):

? *The British **media** at its [✓ their] finest is [✓ are] the best in the world.*

? *The **media** doesn't [✓ don't] cover that sort of abuse any more.*

This usage has even extended to another meaning of *media*, where it is distinctly incongruous:

✗ *Electronic* **media** *does* [✓ *do*], *however, offer very great opportunities for the enlightened corporate records manager.*

But there is still some opposition to this development,
because unlike data, which is very generalized in sense,
behind *media* there is still a sense of identifiable
elements (the press, radio, television, and so on). For
this reason it is preferable to regard *media* as a plural
noun, which is never wrong and often makes much
better sense (as well as better grammar):

✓ *The* **media** *tend to promote individuals in this last group.*
✓ *When the* **media** *report events there must always be a line,
an angle, a spin.*
✓ *On neither occasion were the* **media** *at all interested in
covering the good news.*

mitigate / militate

Parliament and the courts have intervened to **mitigate** *the
harshness of the situation.*
Their presence **militated** *against a relaxed and restful
environment.*

These words are often confused because their sound
and rhythm are close, and both have meanings to do
with reducing things. *Mitigate* is a transitive verb (i.e.
it takes an object) and means 'to make less severe',
whereas *militate* is intransitive, is followed by *against*,
and means 'to counteract, to have an effect against'.

momentarily

Momentarily, like *presently*, has a different range of meanings in British and American English, and the pronunciation also differs: the stress is on the first syllable (*mo-ment-*) in Britain and on the third (*-ar-i-ly*) in America.

In British usage, it means 'for a moment' or 'briefly':

*I was afraid to leave Edinburgh, even **momentarily**, in case there was word from the War Office.*
*Mandy seemed **momentarily** at a loss for words.*
*The sky was **momentarily** lit with pink and green light.*

In American usage it has the same meaning and also the meaning 'at any moment, very shortly':

*We shall be landing **momentarily** in Chicago.*
*The British will secure Cormack's release **momentarily.***

This meaning is creeping into British use, and the word is best avoided in contexts where either meaning could be understood, causing ambiguity.

> *'I shall deal with the matter momentarily,' he said. It was a good word. It always made people hesitate. They were never quite sure whether he meant he'd deal with it* now, *or just deal with it* briefly.

> Terry Pratchett, *Guards! Guards!*, 1997

mutual

Many usage guides warn against using *mutual* to mean 'common' as in Dickens' title *Our Mutual Friend* (a novel first published in 1864). Properly used, it should

imply a degree of two-way action rather than just
sharing:

*We agreed to give each other **mutual** support.*
*The kiss they shared was a **mutual** one.*

But the notion is hard to pin down, and human
relationships cannot always be compartmentalized in
this way. As long as there is an element of interaction
in the sharing notion, *mutual* is an acceptable word to
use:

✓ *They had come to have a friendly discussion about a matter
in which he might have a **mutual** interest.*
✓ *We tramped upstairs and enjoyed a **mutual** moan about
why hospitals always put the sickest patients in the most
inaccessible places.*

Common would do in place of *mutual* in the first
sentence but not in the second. Its usefulness as an
alternative is further limited by the ambiguity it can
often pose:

✓ *They discovered they had a **mutual** acquaintance in the
accounts office.*
? *They discovered they had a **common** [= 'shared' or 'vulgar'?]
acquaintance in the accounts office.*

The same applies to the adverb *mutually*, but here there
is usually a stronger element of interaction supplied by
the word it qualifies:

✓ *It would be best to fix a regular **mutually** agreeable day for
visiting.*

✓ Suicide and anorexia are by no means **mutually** exclusive phenomena.

✓ It is essential that relationships between education and clinical staff are **mutually** supportive.

> The routine of camp life threw them much together, and mutual esteem soon grew into a bond of mutual good fellowship.
>
> Louisa M Alcott, *On Picket Duty*, 1864

of *in* must of, should of, etc.

✗ Somebody **must of** [✓ must have] thrown it out then.

✗ You **should of** [✓ should have] got some more fromage frais.

Using *of* instead of *have* after *must*, *should*, *would*, and other auxiliary verbs is regarded by many as a sure sign of illiteracy. Its use arises from the similarity of sound in rapid speech, but it should never be translated into writing or print in this form.

ongoing

✓ The organization offers them vital **ongoing** support.

This is a word with a bad reputation, but it has begun to lose its vogue status and can be useful. It is not always satisfactorily replaced by *continuing*, *developing*, and other alternatives.

But *ongoing* jars with many readers as an unattractive neologism, and if you think your readers might bridle at it, you can often avoid using it. The alternatives – including rephrasing – can be just as effective if you want to be more straightforward:

? *Investing companies have found that there is an* **ongoing** [✓ *constant* or *current*] *need for training and retraining.*

? *If your problem is* **ongoing** [✓ *If your problem persists*], *ask your doctor to refer you to a dermatologist.*

? *She had just signed a new one-year shoe contract with the company as part of its* **ongoing** [✓ *continuing*] *support for British tennis.*

ought

There are two important points to bear in mind when using *ought*:

• Because *ought* is a modal verb it can form a negative directly with *not*, and it doesn't need the support of *do*:

Education **ought not** *to have an end.*

• However, *ought* has no past form and cannot even form one with *do*. Instead, the tense is expressed by the accompanying verb (*be* in the example below):

I **ought to have been** *more careful.*

It is ungrammatical to write *did ought*, and *didn't ought*, though more common, is even worse:

✗ *I* **didn't ought** *to ask her* [✓ *ought not to have asked her*], *but I did anyway.*

partly / partially

Choice between *partly* and *partially* causes a lot of trouble, because their meanings overlap and people are aware of subtle differences. There is a convenient rule of thumb. If you think of *partly* as the opposite of *wholly* or *entirely*, and *partially* as the opposite of *completely*, both words tend to fall into place. Compare the following two sentences:

*The house is **partly** timbered.*
*The house is **partially** timbered.*

The first version means that timbering is a feature of part of the house (i.e. it is not *wholly* timbered), whereas the second means that the timbering has yet to be finished (i.e. it is not *completely* timbered).

   This rule works reasonably well, but because there is a general preference for *partly*, it tends to intrude on the meaning identified for *partially*:

*He was **partly** educated in Bologna.*
*Her masts and sails were splintered, torn, and **partly** missing.*
*The site was once an ancient meeting place and was **partly** excavated.*
*Amalfi Cathedral has been **partly** rebuilt but still has its beautiful campanile and eleventh-century doors.*

Here are a few more guidelines that might help:

• *Partly* works better when it applies to a whole sentence or idea:

*Perhaps **partly** it was my fault.*

• There is the added complication that *partially* has another meaning, the opposite of *impartially*, which can get in the way:

? *He was **partially** educated* [could = educated in a prejudiced way] *in Bologna.*

? *This bias was no doubt at least **partially*** [could = unfairly] *a reflection of the haphazard organization of policing in Britain at the beginning of the 19th century.*

• *Partly* is generally preferred in contrastive uses where it is repeated:

*I felt a tremor that was **partly** apprehension and **partly** excitement.*

• Where the meaning is 'up to a point', *partially* is often better immediately before an adjective:

*As likely as not they were cottagers **partially** dependent on casual labouring.*
*You could finish up at least **partially** buried if there was a cave-in.*
*McBride, who is **partially** deaf, was attacked by two youths when only yards from his home.*
*The statue is a **partially** draped Aphrodite of the first century* AD.

presently

This is a word to be careful with, as its meaning differs in British and American English, and the American use has begun to impinge on the British. The traditional British meaning is 'in a while, soon':

Presently he trudged on, alone and wretched.
*I shall phone her **presently**.*

The American meaning (which was formerly also used in British English) is 'at present, now', and normally refers to the time of utterance:

*Their fees and expenses **presently** stand at £69m.*

The context, and in particular the tense (past, present, or future) of the verb, usually makes it clear which meaning is intended.

quite

*It is after all **quite** difficult to remember exactly what it felt like to be a small person.*

The problem with *quite* is that it has two meanings that merge into one another in a way that makes it hard to be sure of the intention. In the sentence given above, *quite* probably means 'fairly' or 'somewhat'; which is its main meaning in modern usage. But *quite* has another meaning, 'fully' or 'completely', as in *have you quite finished?* In some cases the context makes it clear which aspect of *quite* is intended:

*The gardens formed another part of the estate, **quite** [= completely] separate from the houses.*
*It must have been **quite** a sacrifice [= a major sacrifice] for both of them to make.*

In other cases the intended sense can be unclear:

*He hummed and sounded **quite** at ease.*
*A small bag of sand did the job **quite** nicely.*

When used with a negative word (*not*, *never*, etc.) the meaning is '[not] completely' or '[not] entirely':

*She is just **not quite** running at her best.*
*He was **never quite** sure why he had married her at all.*

If by using *quite* you create a possible doubt in your readers, it is best to use an alternative word, such as *completely*, *entirely*, *fully*, or *utterly* in the first sense and *fairly*, *rather*, or *somewhat* in the second sense.

rather than

The phrase *rather than* is used to mean 'instead of' or 'in preference to', and this variation in emphasis has a bearing on the way it is used. When it is followed by a noun there is no problem:

*I drink tea **rather than** coffee.*

The problems begin with pronouns, which change their form. Do you say *rather than me* or *rather than I*? The answer is to be guided by the word that comes before *rather*:

*I wanted to see **her** rather than **him**.*
***She**, rather than **he**, was the person I wanted to see.*

If a noun comes before *rather* and a pronoun is needed after it, you can determine which pronoun to use after it by substituting a pronoun for the noun. For example:

*I want to speak to **Hamish** rather than **she/her**.*

The pronoun in place of *Hamish* would be *him*: and so the following pronoun would be *her*:

*I want to speak to **him** rather than **her**.*

So the correct form in the original sentence is *her*:

*I want to speak to **Hamish** rather than **her**.*

(The same applies to alternatives such as *instead of* or *and not*, which could be used in these sentences in place of *rather than*.)

   You may feel even more confused when verbs are involved: do you use an *-ing* form after *rather than* or a simple form of the verb?

*She spoke quietly and calmly, **rather than** shout/shouting at them.*

The answer is to use an *-ing* form when the meaning tends to be 'instead of', i.e. when the second alternative is rejected or did not happen. In the previous sentence, *rather than* introduces an action that was not performed (she did not shout at them, she spoke quietly and calmly), and so the choice would be:

*She spoke quietly and calmly, **rather than** shouting at them.*

Here are some more examples to illustrate the point further:

*Being a backbench Member of Parliament rounded off his life **rather than** offering a springboard for future achievement.* (it did not offer a springboard)
*We played positionally **rather than** going for an all-out assault.* (we did not go for an all-out assault)
*He strode on ahead, **rather than** waiting for her to join him.* (he did not wait for her)

You use the simple form of the verb that follows *rather than* when there is a sense of balance between the alternatives and the choice is a matter of preference rather than rejection:

*He had suffered hardship **rather than** ask his family for money.*
*We'd gone past by then so **rather than** reverse we turned round further on.*

(It's true in these sentences that he didn't ask his family for money and we didn't reverse, but these options are offered as potential rather than rejected alternatives. We could substitute *asking* and *reversing*, which would emphasize the rejection of the alternatives much more strongly.)

If the verb that precedes *rather than* has a special form, e.g. if it is itself an *-ing* participle or an *-ed* participle or a *to*-infinitive, the verb that follows tends to follow suit:

*The objective is to escape from an uncomfortable position **rather than** to reach a particular destination.*
*I decided to stay overnight **rather than** wait for the last bus home.*
*They will be focusing on attracting a new customer base **rather than** wooing an old one.*
*Liz was humiliated by this, **rather than** enraged.*

the reason is . . .

✘ *The second reason is because [✓ that] it would put an intolerable burden of security on us.*

When *reason* is followed by *be* and a clause, the linking word should be *that* and not *because*. The reason for this is that the notion of 'because' is already implied in the word *reason*. (Note the last sentence!)

replace *and* substitute

These words, which are complementary in meaning, sometimes present an uncertainty of choice between *by* and *with* as the link word. The general pattern is:

- A replaces B
- You replace B **with** A
- B is replaced **by** or **with** A
- You substitute A **for** B
- A is substituted **for** B

*A security switch **replaces** the existing light switch.*
*Remove the fitting using a blowtorch, and **replace** it **with** a compression joint.*
*Hoare resigned, to be **replaced by** Anthony Eden.*
*When an initiative is taken away, there is always the hope that it will be **replaced with** another.*
*Parliament itself could **substitute** an act **for** an earlier one.*
*A machine had been **substituted for** the original human partner in the dialogue.*

respective *and* respectively

These are useful words when two or more items, whether named separately or collectively, need to be distinguished, in the order in which they occur, in relation to what is said about them later in the sentence:

*It has taken several years of animated discussions among the members and their **respective** lawyers.*

(Use of *respective* shows that each member had his or her own lawyer. Without it we might think that the members were represented collectively by a group of lawyers rather than individually by different lawyers.)

*MPs protested that news from their **respective** areas of the country was not being heard.*

(Each MP belonged to a different area; they didn't all share a group of areas.)

*The two men were charged with assault and grievous bodily harm **respectively**.*

(Use of *respectively* shows that one of the men was charged with assault and the other with grievous bodily harm. Without it we might think that both men were charged with both offences.)

*Gravity and magnetic lineaments are shown in yellow and green **respectively**.*

(Gravity is shown in yellow and magnetic lineaments in green, not both in green and yellow.)

*The class was asked to instruct me and one of the pupils in how to behave as a reporter and doctor **respectively**, the reporter wanting information from the doctor about 'these new machines' he had heard about.*

(The speaker took the role of reporter and the pupil that of doctor; without *respectively* we might think that both people were instructed in both roles.)

In other cases, *respective* and *respectively* (the first more usually than the second) can be redundant because the sense is clear without them:

✗ *Each parent had applied for his **respective** daughter to be admitted to the school.* (*Each* already individualizes the parents.)

✗ *These companies all had able and high-calibre people who knew their **respective** businesses very well.*

✗ *Both men built exactly the same design of fruit house in their **respective** gardens.*

✗ *Two practical skills day events are planned in Glasgow, for 21st April and 20th October **respectively**.*

Sometimes *respective(ly)* can be justified logically (and makes for a better sentence balance) but the context makes the meaning obvious and it can be left out:

? *His sons Alfred and Albert were sixteen and nineteen **respectively**.*

? *The UK and US embassies urged their **respective** nationals to leave the country.*

tight / tightly

Like *flat* (see p. 253) *tight* has two adverb forms: *tight* and *tightly*. *Tight* is used with a number of verbs, especially in commands (*hold tight, sit tight, sleep tight*), and in a number of compound adjectives (*tight-fisted, tight-fitting, tight-knit, tight-lipped, tight shut*).

In general use, *tightly* is the correct form:

*Her arms went around him and she held him **tightly**.*
*These devices fit **tightly** between the window and its frame.*
*He held out his hand, but Claudia kept hers **tightly** clenched at her side.*

transpire

Transpire is based on a Latin word meaning 'to breathe', and its correct meaning is 'to leak out, to become known'. It should not be used as an alternative for *occur* or *happen*:

✓ It **transpired** that Hannah was well capable of coping with this sudden celebrity status.

✓ The two girls, it **transpired**, did not work in a cabaret but assisted at a gambling salon.

✗ Nothing so romantic ever **transpired** [✓ happened or occurred] there.

✗ When Slaughter told me what had **transpired** [✓ happened or occurred or taken place], I had the lass brought here to my lodgings.

unique

? The Sheraton is fairly **unique** in having a complex of this size attached to it.

A sentence like this raises eyebrows: surely, if *unique* means 'not like any other person or thing', something is either unique or not, and so nothing can be *fairly* unique. Nor, for that matter, can it be *rather unique* or *somewhat unique*, let alone *very unique* or *extremely unique*. But this objection is based on logic and not grammar; it is philosophical rather than linguistic. Linguistically, it is still idiomatic to qualify *unique*, as with *perfect* and other theoretically absolute concepts:

All original fittings were refurbished, which makes the car **so unique**.

*For most of the plant's life, it just looks like a stem, but if you catch it at the right time, it unfolds beautiful bright yellow petals and is **rather unique**.*

> *'A very unique child,' thought I, as I viewed her*
> *sleeping countenance by the fitful moonlight.*
>
> Charlotte Brontë, *Villette*, 1853

until *and* till

Till is not a shortening of *until* but is the older word; the *un-* element is an intensifying prefix meaning 'up to' or 'as far as'. The two words are largely interchangeable both as prepositions and as conjunctions, but there are a few special points to note:

• *Until* is more usual at the beginning of a sentence:

Until they arrive there's not much we can do.

• *Till* is most effective when followed by a simple noun:

*Stephen worked on the armchairs **till** lunchtime.*

• *Till* has a more informal tone, especially when used as a conjunction (followed by a clause with a verb) and *until* is often preferred for this reason:

*It took a period of years **till** they got it finalized.*
*Philip waited **till** he couldn't see him any more.*
*A meeting should wait **until** we have a programme.*
*She kept her host in conversation **until** two in the morning.*

very / much

Very and *much* are both used as intensifying adverbs, and their roles are complementary. *Very* qualifies adjectives and adverbs: *very angry, very large, very unusually*. *Much* qualifies the past participles of verbs used as adjectives, especially when they come before a noun: *a much enlarged edition, a much complained-of decision*.

There is, however, a considerable grey area because some past participles have largely lost their verbal association and become adjectives in their own right, e.g. *annoyed, pleased, tired*, and *worried*. In these cases *very* is the usual qualifier to use: *very annoyed* and *very tired* are idiomatic forms whereas *much annoyed* sounds dated and *much tired* is simply not English any more.

Other cases are more borderline and offer you a choice. For example, *a much honoured politician* implies a continuing process, whereas *a very honoured politician* suggests the current state of affairs.

The following examples all imply processes, with the verb aspect predominant:

*Erato launched its series with tributes to two **much loved** French musicians.*
*She is **much exercised** about a letter which arrived today.*
*One aspect of illusion is perspective, **much valued** in the Western tradition.*

The following examples all imply states, with the adjective aspect predominant:

*These roles are **very limited**.*
*He felt **very involved** in the affair.*
*The sound is **very distorted**.*

Glossary

This glossary includes the terms most often used in the course of this book. Other terms can be found in the main text by referring to the index.

absolute   an absolute adjective is one used without a following noun, e.g. *the poor*.

abstract noun   a noun that names an abstract quality, state, or activity, e.g. *anger, hunting, loneliness, statement, warmth*. See also **Concrete noun**.

active   the form of a verb in which the subject performs the action and the object (if any) is affected by the action, e.g. *She parked the car; A man stood in the doorway*. See also **Passive**.

adjective   a word that describes a person or thing, e.g. *a red hat, an Italian meal, the room is square*.

adverb   a word that tells you how or where or when an action is done, e.g. *She smiled gently; He went downstairs; Tomorrow we'll go swimming*.

adverbial
***or* adverb phrase**   a phrase that has the role of an adverb, e.g. *down the road, in the morning, in any way you can*.

affirmative   an affirmative verb or sentence states a fact that is the case, or is equivalent to the answer 'yes'. See also **Negative**.

agreement   use of the correct forms of words when they relate to each other in a sentence, e.g. changing *have* to *has* in the sentence *He has a lot to answer for.*

ambiguity   using words in a way that can produce more than one possible meaning, e.g. *Will you check their progress?*

attributive   an attributive adjective or noun is one that is placed before another word, typically a noun, so as to qualify it in some way, e.g. *a bright moon, an expiry date.* See also **Predicative**.

auxiliary verbs   the verbs *be, do,* and *have,* and the modal verbs *can, could, may, might, must, shall, should, will,* and *would,* all of which are used to make forms of other verbs, e.g. *be going, do like, have seen, can sleep,* etc.

clause   a group of words containing a verb and its subject. A main clause makes sense by itself and can form a complete sentence, e.g. *I'll write them a letter.* A subordinate clause does not make complete sense by itself and is attached to a main clause, e.g. *I'll write them a letter if I have the time.*

collective noun   a noun that refers to a group of individual people or things, e.g. *audience, body, committee, government, team,* etc.

comparative   the form of an adjective or adverb ending in *-er* or preceded by *more,* e.g. *larger, happier, more safely.* See also **Superlative**.

complement   a word or phrase that completes a sentence in some way, other than the subject, verb, and object, e.g. *librarian* in *They made her librarian* and *delighted* in *He is delighted.*

complex sentence   a sentence with a main clause and one or more subordinate clauses linked by a conjunction, e.g. *Read this article when you have a chance.*

compound sentence   a sentence with more than one main clause linked by a conjunction, e.g. *Read this article and tell me what you think of it.*

concrete noun   a noun that refers to a physical object, e.g. *ceiling, person, truck.* See also **Abstract noun.**

conjunction   a word that links other words or groups of words, e.g. *and, but, if, unless, whether.*

consonant   any of the letters that are not vowels: *b, c, d, f, g, h, j, k, l, m, n, p, q, r, s, t, v, w, x, y* (e.g. in *yellow*), *z.*

countable noun   a noun that can form plurals, e.g. *bus, crisis, remark, kindness* = a kind act. See also **Mass noun, Uncountable noun.**

determiner   a word that comes before a noun and limits its meaning in some way, e.g. *a, the, this, some, each,* etc.

direct speech   speech that gives the actual words used, normally in quotation marks, e.g. *He said, 'You will be late.'* See also **Indirect speech.**

ellipsis   the omission of certain words without loss of meaning, e.g. of *that* in the sentence *He told us [that] we would be late.*

finite   a finite form of a verb is one that is used in a particular tense, person, and number, e.g. *sat* in *They **sat** down* (as distinct from the base form *sit*).

future tense   the form of a verb that indicates an action or state still to come, e.g. *We **will be** there.*

future per-   the form of a verb, typically formed with *shall*
fect tense   *have* or *will have*, that indicates an action or state that will be completed in relation to a point of time in the future, e.g. *By tomorrow they **will have arrived**.*

gender   a classification into masculine, feminine, and neuter. There is very little grammatical gender left in English, apart from the pronouns (*he, she, it, his, her,* etc.), some occupational nouns in *-ess* and *-ette*, and a few special nouns, e.g. *widow, widower; hero, heroine.*

gradable   a gradable adjective is one that can vary in intensity and be qualified by words such as *fairly, rather, very, more, less,* etc., e.g. *big, difficult, heavy.*

indirect   a question put in a reported form (see **Indirect**
question   **speech** below), e.g. *He asked where the bathroom was; I wonder who that can be.*

indirect   speech in which the words used are reported
speech   by someone other than the original speaker, with a reporting verb such as *say, remark, tell,* etc., and with the tense and grammar of the words modified to suit this, e.g. *He **told** us we **would** be late.* See also **Direct speech**.

infinitive   the form of a word without any subject or inflection, e.g. *say* as distinct from *says* or *said*. An infinitive can either be unaccompanied (a bare infinitive, e.g. *I will **say***) or be preceded by *to* (a *to*-infinitive, e.g. *I want **to say***).

inflection   the change in the forms of words to suit their role in the sentence, e.g. by adding -*s* to the third person singular of verbs (e.g. *comes, says*) or to form the plurals of nouns (e.g. *cakes, comments*) or by adding -*ed* or -*ing* to form the past or present participle.

interjection   an exclamation such as *ah!, alas!, oops!*

interrogative   an interrogative word or sentence is one that asks a question, e.g. *Are you ready?*; *Which car shall we take?*

intransitive   an intransitive verb, or meaning of a verb, is one that does not have a grammatical object, e.g. *The door **opened**.* See also **Transitive**.

main clause   a part of a sentence, containing a verb, that makes complete sense by itself. See also **Clause**.

main verb   the verb in a main clause.

mass noun   a noun that is normally singular only, but unlike fully uncountable nouns can form plurals in the special sense 'an amount of', e.g. *beer* (*three beers*) or 'a type of', e.g. *cheese* (*try different cheeses*). See also **Countable noun, Uncountable noun**.

modal verbs   the verbs *can, could, may, might, must, shall, should, will,* and *would*, which are used to form moods (modes of expression denoting a fact, command, possibility, etc.) of other verbs. They can form negatives and questions without the help of *do*, they do not add -*s* in the third person singular, and they do not have an infinitive form.

modifier a word, typically an adjective, that describes or modifies a noun in some way, e.g. *cold tea, coffee table*).

negative a negative word or sentence denies that a fact is the case, typically by using words such as *no, not, never*, etc., or is equivalent to the answer 'no'. See also **Affirmative**.

noun a word that refers to a person or thing, e.g. *cat, health, sugar, Henry, Paris*. See also **Abstract noun, Concrete noun, Proper noun; Countable noun, Mass noun, Uncountable noun; Collective noun**.

number the grammatical categorization of nouns and other words as **Singular** or **Plural**.

object the person or thing that is affected by the action of an active transitive verb, e.g. *Susan opened the door*.

objective the form of a word when it is the object of a verb or follows a preposition, especially of a pronoun, e.g. *me* and *her* instead of *I* and *she*. See also **Subjective**.

part of speech a category based on the role that a word has in a sentence. The traditional parts of speech are noun, verb, adjective, adverb, pronoun, preposition, conjunction, and interjection.

participle see **Past participle, Present participle**.

passive the form of a verb in which the object of the action becomes the subject of the verb and the performer of the action is either not expressed or expressed after *by*, e.g. *The car **was parked** by her*. See also **Active**.

past participle a form of a verb typically ending in *-ed* or *-t* (e.g. *danced, caught*) used to form past tenses and the passive voice.

past perfect (or pluperfect) tense a form of a verb, typically formed with *had*, denoting a state or action that is completed in relation to a point of reference in the past, e.g. *We had been waiting an hour when the bus finally came.*

past tense the form of a verb that indicates an action or state in the past, e.g. *We were there.*

perfect tense a form of a verb, typically formed with *have* or *has*, that refers to a past action or state in the context of the present, e.g. *I wonder if they have ever been to Paris.*

person a categorization of words according to whether the person or thing referred to is the speaker (first person, corresponding to the pronouns *I* and *me*), a person addressed (second person, corresponding to *you*), or another person or thing (third person, corresponding to *he, she, it, they*, or a noun).

phrasal verb a combination of a verb and an adverb such as *off* and *up*, usually having a special meaning, e.g. *take off, give up*. An object of the verb can come between it and the adverb, e.g. *take your jacket off.*

phrase a group of words forming a grammatical unit but normally without a verb and not making complete sense by itself. A noun phrase (e.g. *the man in the moon*) is equivalent to a noun, an adverb phrase (e.g. *by the river*) is equivalent to an adverb, and so on.

plural a form of a noun, pronoun, or verb that refers to more than one individual (e.g. *cats, crises, people*). See also **Singular**.

postpositive a modifier that comes after the noun it qualifies, e.g. *president elect, money galore*.

predicate the part of a sentence other than the subject, typically including a verb, object, and any adverb phrases, e.g. *The man took a note out of his wallet.*

predicative a predicative adjective is one that is placed in the predicate of a sentence, typically after the verb, e.g. *The door is red* as distinct from *the red door*. See also **Attributive**.

preposition a word that shows position in relation to space or time, e.g. *after* as in *after dinner, in, on, to, with*, etc.

present participle a form of a verb ending in *-ing* (e.g. *dancing, catching*) used to form continuous tenses and verbal adjectives (e.g. *annoying, surprising*).

present tense the form of a verb that refers to present time, e.g. *We are here.*

pronoun a word that is used in place of a noun: *he, she, it, they, this, those*, etc.

proper noun a noun that refers to a particular individual, e.g. *Everest, New York, Concorde*. The term is sometimes extended to include personal names, e.g. *David, Rebecca*.

quantifier a type of modifier that indicates quantity, e.g. *some, a few, many*, etc.

relative clause	a clause introduced by *that, which, who*, or *whose*, e.g. *The person **who was here** has gone*; *The animal **that you saw** was a goat*.
sentence	a group of words containing a main clause, typically with a verb, making complete sense by itself, and not linked grammatically to any larger structure.
sentence adverb	an adverb that qualifies a whole statement, e.g. *Clearly there had been a mistake*.
simple sentence	a sentence consisting of a single main clause, e.g. *I am reading a book*. See also **Complex sentence**, **Compound sentence**.
singular	a form of a noun, pronoun, or verb that refers to one individual (e.g. *cat, crisis, person*) or to the only form of an uncountable noun (e.g. *happiness, sugar*). See also **Plural**.
split infinitive	a *to*-infinitive in which a word, typically an adverb or adverb phrase, comes between *to* and the verb, e.g. *to really mean it*.
stress	the part of a word that is emphasized more than the others, e.g. the first syllable in *matrimony* and the third in *matrimonial*.
subject	the person or thing that performs the action of an active verb (e.g. ***Susan** opened the door*) or is affected by the action of a passive verb (e.g. ***The door** was opened by Susan*).
subjective	the form of a word, especially of a pronoun, when it is the subject of a verb, e.g. *I* and *she*. See also **Objective**.
subjunctive	a special form of a verb, in English now limited

to certain expressions of wish or command and usually noticeable only in the third person singular which does not end in -s, e.g. *God save the Queen*; *perish the thought*.

subordinate clause a clause that is not a main clause but is attached to the main clause of a sentence with a word such as *if, whether, who, which,* or *that.* See also **Clause**.

superlative the form of an adjective or adverb ending in -*est* or preceded by *most*, e.g. *largest, happiest, most safely*. See also **Comparative**.

syllable a unit of pronunciation that is uninterrupted and contains a vowel: there are three syllables in the word *hap-pi-ness*.

tense the categorization of verbs according to whether the action or state is in the present, past, or future. See also **Past tense, Present tense, Future tense**.

that-clause a clause introduced by *that*, e.g. *He knew **that I was wrong**.* The word *that* can often be omitted, e.g. *He knew I was wrong*.

to-infinitive an infinitive of a verb with the word *to* preceding it, e.g. *They wanted **to leave**.*

transitive a transitive verb, or meaning of a verb, is one that has a grammatical object, e.g. *She **opened** the door.* See also **Intransitive**.

uncountable noun a noun that does not form a plural, e.g. *poverty, traffic, wealth.* See also **Mass noun, Countable noun**.

verb a word that refers to an action (e.g. *go, lie, send*) or state (e.g. *be, exist, remain*).

verbal noun a form of a verb ending in *-ing* used as a noun, e.g. *dancing is fun.*

vowel any of the letters *a, e, i, o,* and *u.* The letter *y* is also classed as a vowel in words such as *rhythm* and *byte.*

***wh*- word** a word such as *who, what, which, when, where, why,* used to ask questions (e.g. **Where** *have you been?*) and to introduce subordinate clauses (e.g. *I don't know* **what** *you mean; They wanted to know* **why** *I had come*).

wordclass another term for **Part of speech**.

Further reading

This is a list of books that will give you further information about points discussed in this book, including some that are touched on only briefly here (such as plain English and punctuation). They are arranged in chronological order of publication:

Fowler, H W and F G, *The King's English* (3rd edition, Oxford University Press, 1931: still in print and still a valuable guide, despite its age)

Gowers, Sir Ernest, *The Complete Plain Words* (3rd edition, HMSO, 1986, and Penguin Books, 1987)

Allen, Robert, *Pocket Fowler's Modern English Usage* (Oxford University Press, 1999; reprinted in paperback, 2002: a modern version in shorter form of the classic book by H W Fowler)

Blamires, Harry, *The Penguin Guide to Plain English* (Penguin Books, 2000)

Ritter, R M, *The Oxford Dictionary for Writers and Editors* (2nd edition, Oxford University Press, 2000: an alphabetical listing of words, phrases, and names that have problems of style or spelling or other special features; now much larger and less handy than the original edition)

Seely, John, *Everyday Grammar* (Oxford University Press, 2001)

Trask, R L, *Mind the Gaffe: The Penguin Guide to Common Errors in English* (Penguin Books, 2001)

Cutts, Martin, *The Oxford Guide to Plain English* (2nd edition, Oxford University Press, 2004)

There are also two volumes on related aspects of writing English in this series of Writers' Guides: *Improve Your Spelling* and *How to Punctuate*, both by George Davidson.

It is important to have a good up-to-date dictionary always to hand: among the best are the *Concise Oxford Dictionary* (11th edition, Oxford University Press, 2004), the *Penguin English Dictionary* (revised edition, Penguin Books, 2003), and *The Chambers Dictionary* (9th edition, Chambers, 2003).

Index

I Subjects

Common terms such as *noun*, *verb*, *plural*, and *sentence* occur throughout the book and in these cases only key references are given. References in bold type are to the Glossary.

II Words and phrases

References to words and phrases used in the tables are marked
with asterisks (*).